Roberto Michels'

FIRST LECTURES IN POLITICAL SOCIOLOGY

Roberto Michels'

FIRST LECTURES IN
POLITICAL SOCIOLOGY

TRANSLATED, WITH AN INTRODUCTION BY

Alfred de Grazia

UNIVERSITY OF MINNESOTA PRESS, Minneapolis
LONDON · GEOFFREY CUMBERLEGE · OXFORD UNIVERITY PRESS

Table of Contents

Introduction BY ALFRED DE GRAZIA   3

CHAPTER I. The Origins of Economic Determinism and
Social Class Theories   10

*Economic Determinism, 10. The Class Struggle, 14. Marx and
Pareto, 18.*

CHAPTER II. The Relation of Economic Events to Personality and Politics   24

*Economic Man, 24. Economics and the Sociology of Religion, 33.
Political Economy and National Politics, 38.*

CHAPTER III. The Elite   63

*The Old Aristocratic Elements of the Elite, 63. The Absorption of
New Elements by the Hereditary Aristocracy, 75. The Elite and
the Proletariat, 80.*

CHAPTER IV. Democratic and Aristocratic Tendencies in
Modern Politics   88

*The Emergence of the Mass Factor in Politics, 88. The Formation
of the Economic Elite, 92.*

CHAPTER V. Social Metabolism and Postwar Events   103

*The Character of Social Change, 103. The Elements of the Political
Class, 106.*

CHAPTER VI. Charismatic Leadership   119

CHAPTER VII. The Sociological Character of Political
Parties   134

*Kinds of Political Parties, 134. The Democratic Appeals, 143. False
Party Classifications, 146.*

Errata

Page 10, line 1, for third read fourteenth
Page 10, line 19, for G. B. read J. B.
Page 23, note 27, for Jahrbuch für Gesetzgebung, Verwaltung read Jahrbuch
für Gesetzgebung, Verwaltung und Volkswirtschaft
Page 23, note 31, for Livingstone read Livingston
Page 52, line 20, for Walter read Ernst
Page 92, line 34, for seventeenth read eighteenth
Page 102, note 38, for 1903 read 1923
Page 133, note 16, for Monarchie, absolue Gouverment, read Monarchie
absolue, Gouvernement,

Roberto Michels'

FIRST LECTURES IN POLITICAL SOCIOLOGY

Introduction

THE materials of political science are so vast in scope and unlimited in detail as to depress a beginning student in search of generalities. Yet his political studies may benefit from an early understanding of certain key ideas. It is to political sociology that we may resort for this purpose, for political sociology treats of the social foundations of politics. It asks and gives answers to a number of questions the essential comprehension of which is the preliminary to further study of political behavior, political institutions, and public law.

Among the basic questions it considers are: What is the relation between economics and politics? How do economics, politics, and religious ideologies interact and affect one another? To what extent does the social configuration of society—its classes, occupations, and levels of opportunity—permeate and condition political activities? Where does political power reside and how is it wielded? What general social changes are occurring and what political changes are associated with them? And who are the political leaders and what are their origins?

Possessed of general answers to these questions, even though they be valid only for the time being, a student of political science gains certain advantages. He can reject or shed a volume of the data that crowds him from all quarters, holding it to be irrelevant or superfluous. He can relate the data he retains to categories which are intellectually useful and capable of being remembered. He can guard himself against the dangers of one-sidedness, the curse of narrowly trained and formally preoccupied minds. He can congratulate himself that he is being realistic, escaping the accusing "qu'importe?" of critical laymen and scholars alike. He can, in sum, feel a little more secure as he moves into the con-stricted quarters of his chosen field of specialization.

The work of Roberto Michels to follow is well-suited to introduce the student to political sociology. He begins by tracing the concept of economic determinism from its earliest manifestations through its development at the hands of Karl Marx and its critique by Vilfredo Pareto and others. He then analyzes the sources of political behavior in a combination of political, economic, social, and ideational factors. Max Weber's famous theory on the relation of religion to economic behavior is discussed. The effects of political decisions on domestic and international economy are revealed. The idea of "economic man," so controversial in social science, is aptly explored and delimited.

Michels then moves into another set of ideas surrounding the concept of the "elite." Here we find new materials to develop and modify the conception first introduced to polit-ical sociology by Gaetano Mosca and Vilfredo Pareto. Mosca had originally attacked the classical theory—put forward by Aristotle, Plato, Vico, and many others—of the division of the forms of government into three: democracy, aristocracy, and tyranny. Real governments do not conform in practice to the legal theory, he wrote. That is, rather than govern-ments actually being governed by the many, the few, or the one, they were in fact always governed by a few. This was the "political class," the "ruling class," or the "elite." It might be ultimately overthrown in the name of the many, the few, or the one, but in reality it would only be replaced by another elite. Pareto, affirming the same condition from his study of history, devoted considerable attention to the phenomenon of "the circulation of elites," the process whereby an old and decadent ruling group is evicted by a new one, possessing qualities and skills essential to the new social situation.

Michels, in this work, describes these theories and carries them along to a new stage of development. He demonstrates how, even in violent revolutions, the new ruling group and elements of the old are assimilated and reconciled. The research of Michels in this highly important area of political mobility is some of the most remarkable in a career noted for its penetration of areas unexplored by political sociologists before him. His last article, published a few days after his death, extends his method and tests his theory by applying it to social changes occurring in Western Europe between the two world wars. It appeared in a short-lived review, *Archives de Sociologie*, in 1936, and is presented here in full as Chapter IV.

There follows a brief description of the mass democratic movement of modern times and its founderings on the shoals of dictatorship and socialist theory. Counter to this tendency is the new drive for power of the industrial giants and the disciples of the managerial revolution. The latter derive intellectual stimulus from the theories of Saint-Simon, and their theories are put most challengingly in America in the writings of James Burnham.

Turning from the economic aspects of politics, and the study of elites and social change, Michels introduces his audience to Max Weber's theory of legitimate authority and charismatic leadership. Michels was one of the first to extend the charismatic or personal leader concept to the developing phenomenon of dictators in Europe. The idea of the "Duce" or the "Führerprinzip" is well, even prophetically, analyzed. The democratic appeals of the leader, his messianic qualities, his psychological relationship to the masses, his tightening grip on the state, his megalomanic tendencies, and even the final refusal to bow to disaster and the preference for death in chaos and glory—all are sketched clearly.

In the article on "The Sociological Character of Political Parties" that follows, we are offered a useful typology of modern political parties according to their underlying motivation, together with a brief summary of Michels' central thesis in his magnificent work, *Political Parties: A Sociological Study of the Oligarchical Tendencies of Modern Democracy.*

Michels also expands therein the definition of the type of "elite" party, calling attention for the first time to the "accordion effect," that alternation of democratization of membership and "purges" that has come to be recognized so clearly in one-party states.

Finally there is presented Michels' article on "Patriotism," perhaps the most lucid and penetrating analysis of this phenomenon to be found in the literature on that subject. We owe this translation from the famed German original, which appeared in the *Handwörterbuch der Soziologie*, to Professor Werner Levi of the Department of Political Science at the University of Minnesota and to Ilse Levi.

Thus, glancing at the general contents of the book, we find that, built around the core of introductory lectures which Michels delivered at the University of Rome and which were published in 1927 as *Corso di Sociologia Politica*, we have a concise and vigorous treatment of essential problems in political sociology at the hands of an outstanding political sociologist of the early twentieth century. There parade before the reader the really great European contributors of the last century: Saint-Simon, Karl Marx, Gabriel Tarde, Gaetano Mosca, Vilfredo Pareto, Max Weber, Werner Sombart, Georges Sorel, and many other critics and scholars. Michels presents them authoritatively and always understandably. His merits as lecturer, which won him wide renown in the universities of Germany, Italy, Switzerland, France, Belgium, and America, are apparent in these pages. He can develop a most complex point, without doing it an injustice, in a way that can easily be followed by the reader. At every step, the sociologist, the economist, the psychologist, and the political scientist—for Michels was all of these—intermingle and reinforce each other. His facility in handling historical and sociological materials is most exceptional, and through it all is apparent the rich culture and realism, often ruthless but never arrogant, of a profound scholar.

Michels was of that precious group of men who made all

Europe their home in the first part of this century, whose affections went to no flag but belonged rather to Western culture. He was born to his role; his mother was French and his father a German of an influential manufacturing and military family of Cologne, descended from Italian ancestors. He studied at Paris, Munich, Leipzig, Halle, and Turin. Youthful activities as part of the extreme syndicalist flank of the German Social Democratic party excluded him from academic appointment in Germany. He joined the faculty at the University of Turin, and later became a naturalized citizen of Italy. Despite his opposition to the Kaiser, his affection for German culture did not cease, and he spent a good part of his life advocating a cultural and economic *rapprochement* between North and South. In 1927 Michels lectured in America and presented materials similar to those of this book in a course at the University of Chicago. His broad interests, warm understanding, and impressive character won him many friends among students and faculty alike.

Michels' relationship to European democracy was complex. If one searched his life and writings for his hierarchy of values, I believe one would have to place extreme individualism, even anarchy, first and derive from that his succeeding values. An energetic anti-authoritarianism characterized his earliest life and one finds in his later writings pensive, regretful references to the unattainable ideal of the Jeffersonian or Rousseauian democrat. Alongside this value, perhaps a little less apparent at first in his life, one would place his romanticism, born of his cosmopolitan family background, the wonderful milieu of prewar intellectualism in Europe, and his education, which was steeped in tradition and history.

It was the authoritarianism immanent in absolute mass democracy—the Caesarist tendency—that pulled him up short; and when he considered that the alternative to the "rule of the masses," as demonstrated by his studies, was the rule of the democratic party bureaucrats, he found himself preferring some aristocracy of culture to the aristocracy of trade unionism. The "culture," "class," and "chivalry" elements in his romantic side triumphed against "economic determinism"—Marx's "philosophy of poverty"—and against the inevitable "bureaucratization" of egalitarian democracy.

He remained a believer in democratic ideals, a disbeliever in the possibility of realizing the ideal. In the very last paragraph of *Political Parties*, he wrote:

"The democratic currents of history resemble successive waves. They break ever on the same shoal. They are ever renewed. This enduring spectacle is simultaneously encouraging and depressing. When democracies have gained a certain stage of development, they undergo a gradual transformation, adopting the aristocratic spirit, and in many cases the aristocratic forms, against which at the outset they struggled so fiercely. Now new accusers arise to denounce the traitors; after an era of glorious combats and of inglorious power, they end by fusing with the old dominant class; whereupon once more they are in their turn attacked by fresh opponents who appeal to the name of democracy. It is probable that this cruel game will continue without end."

His reply to the question, "The best government being impossible, what would the best possible government be?" would probably suggest an open aristocracy of culture. The ruling class would be based on elements stretching far into the past, composed of families who knew and respected the values of the culture and had grown relaxed in the enjoyment of them. They would be continually but not too rapidly reinforced and reinvigorated by rising elements founded on wealth (for the wealthy invariably make their way up and undergo cultural training during their ascent), and on ability, men who have acquired merit by means of the bounty and foresight of the older ruling elements. This is essentially the idea of Edmund Burke.

Michels' theory of society reminds one very strongly of James Madison, for both saw the social process as the competition of self-interested factions. They agreed upon values, too, for both felt that society would function best if it allowed and demanded the circulation of the elites and forestalled a monopoly of power by majority or factions. If upon Madison's ideas we were to superimpose those of Henry Adams—nostalgic, fearful of excesses, tradition-proud—then we would come close to describing Michels in terms of the American setting.

My thanks are owing Professors Harold S. Quigley, Werner Levi, and Mulford Q. Sibley for their aid and advice on the manuscript. The editorial assistance of Kenneth G. Olson was continuously valuable. His cooperation and that of Mortimer L. Naftalin and Kurt Shell is gratefully acknowledged. I wish especially to thank my father for his extensive and indispensable help and encouragement in preparing this work. Chapter VII is reprinted from the November 1927 number of the *American Political Science Review* (Vol. XXI, No. 4, pp. 753–72) through the kind permission of the editor, Frederic A. Ogg.

ALFRED DE GRAZIA

CHAPTER I

The Origins of Economic Determinism and Social Class Theories

ECONOMIC DETERMINISM

THE Arab philosopher, Ibn Kaldun, who lived in the third century, may have been the earliest scientific exponent of the economic conception of history. He believed that the leading thread of history lay not in military or political vicissitudes, but rather, as he expresses himself, in man's social state. He means thereby man's degree of civilization, and its causal or concurrent conditions such as barbarism, the improvement of manners, the formation of families, of tribes, and all the various elements of superiority that people acquire in the course of one event or other. From these originate dynasties and empires, social differentiations and lucrative professional occupations (the trades, that is, that give life to man), the sciences, and the arts. Moreover he insisted on the essential thesis that differences in customs and institutions depend on the various ways in which man procures for himself the means of subsistence.[1]

Among the moderns, that is, those who lived after the Renaissance, the first guess at the political urgency and the practical gravity of the problem is, perhaps, that of G. B. Colbert, finance secretary to Louis XIV. Seized by great curiosity to know whether the Romans, so feared, so opulent, and so great, might also have had the richest trade, and if, generally speaking, the wealth of a nation could last without industries, even though it had unbounded political ability, Colbert therefore commissioned the celebrated historian, Bishop Daniel

10

Huet, to write a history of commerce and navigation among the ancients. But the historical treatise of Huet, however learned and interesting, in neglecting through over-systematization the connections between the two phenomena, the historic-economic and the historic-political, did not give the results that might have been expected.

The concept expressed by Ibn Kaldun was not lost, although not a trace of it is found in any of the Eastern or Western philosophers who wrote for centuries after him. Thus, to cite only one example, the Marquis de La Fare, a French gentleman, at the court of Louis XIV, strove to determine the causal chains linking the professions, the social class, and psychology, and cautioned that the mentality of men undergoes fundamental changes, not only in proportion to their state of mind and happiness, but also according to their degree of wealth or poverty. De La Fare, by affirming that "everything partakes of the spirit of its social state" implicitly presented the thesis that ideology is a sort of superstructure of economy. For that reason the princes and the rich would differ substantially from ordinary people. By the same token, the middle-class man and the workingman, the soldier and the merchant, would have dissimilar and opposite ideas, all of them following "l'esprit particulier de leur profession."[2]

Later on, in the epoch of the great technical inventions that "revolutionized" the means of production and brought on that new and powerful social era called the machine age, or also (though the two concepts do not coincide at all) the capitalistic era, a German philosopher, Christian Garve, a disciple of Kant, declared that the phenomenon of social class differentiation surpasses national differentiation in importance. He says that the social factor, at any actual historic moment, is very important, even more than the national factor. Indeed, Garve maintained that the differences between diverse peoples are of less importance than those that separate the various social classes within the structure of the same nation, provided that the relative human inequalities had persisted for a generation or more.[3]

The Englishman Ferguson, who declared in 1776 that any kind of economic occupation produces in man a special mentality and that each single trade "requires different talents and inspires different sentiments,"[4] has been, so far as I know, the first scientist to attempt to study a little more definitely the psychology of the factory worker. He emphasized the damage caused by the monotony of work to those who were continuously performing the same task, and pointed to ignorance as a characteristic of the industrial worker. Is it not ignorance, according to Ferguson, which besides being the mother of superstition, is also the daughter of modern industry? For the masters will receive the most sumptuous income exactly in those branches of industry where the kind of work requires of the worker the least spirit of initiative and where he therefore becomes a mere cog in the machine.[5]

The transformation of the workingman into a living machine had already been forecast by Diderot in a contribution to the *Grande Encyclopédie*,[6] and must also have preoccupied Adam Smith a few years later when he feared that the new technical methods would in the end debase the workingman to the point of his losing interest in his country and its eventual defense.[7] These fears expressed by Smith—and shared earlier for Italy by Verri[8]—concerning the diminishing patriotism of the British workers in the eighteenth century had been encountered in the charge of pusillanimity hurled, more than two centuries ago, by a member of the diplomatic corps of the Serenissima, at the master class of the handicraftsmen and of the merchants of Florence, who, according to the author, were too much addicted to manual and humble labor to face victoriously the dangers of war.[9]

The thesis of machine labor's deleterious effect on the workingman's intelligence became afterward the subject of lively discussion. Some writers, for example MacCulloch, contested the very existence of the phenomenon and asserted that on the contrary the division of labor in the factory makes the workingman increasingly active.[10] Other writers, influenced by Ferguson, Michelet, and others, insisted on the merely mechanical and therefore tedious character of modern labor.[11]

To the latter view Blanqui properly objected that, if it is true that city workers are dull and brutalized, it is no less true that peasants, who do not operate machines, nor do any fractionalized or subdivided work, certainly are not more intelligent.[12] However, most economists, Catholics, socialists, and even liberals who wrote in the first sixty years of the nineteenth century, including Villermé[13] and Tocqueville,[14] developed and deepened the thesis that the irresponsibility and unintelligibility of machine work in industry constituted a fearful incubus for the worker, rendering him liable to apathy and indifference, or to rebellion.

Meanwhile another concept of class, the physiological, had been advanced. This concept dates back to the study of Bernardino Ramazzini on occupational diseases. In a celebrated treatise, published in 1613, the illustrious professor of the University of Padua delineated "the diseases to which the arts expose those that exercise them," and advised doctors to question a patient before proceeding to a diagnosis of his malady on the kind of work he was or had been doing.[15] In 1816 the psychological differentiation of the proletarian types undertaken by Ramazzini was developed by Cadet de Gassicourt in the following terms: "However little one may possess the habit of observing and comparing, it is impossible to survey many factories of the same kind without noting definite similarities not only in looks, in the deportment, in the habits of artisans and in their customs, but even in their physical constitution, their temperament, and their predispositions to certain ailments."[16] In consequence, even a special discipline appeared, intermediate between medicine and social science, a typical *Grenzwissenschaft* or boundary-line science.

In England the revolutionary events of the first half of the sixteenth century produced a school of philosophers of history, the most important of whom were Thomas Hobbes (1589–1679) and James Harrington (1611–1677). Harrington affirmed the existence of a causal connection between the economic conditions of a country and its political constitution, in the sense of a dependence of one on the other.[17] His doctrine found in France during the revolution a congenial successor in Pierre Joseph Marie Barnave of Grenoble, a member of the Constituent Assembly and founder of the Club of Jacobins. In 1791–92, making use of a brief pause in his political activities, he wrote down his thoughts and opinions on the origin of the revolution and seems to have been influenced by the idea of the absolute predominance of economic over political phenomena (*Introduction à la Révolution francaise*).[18]

Early in the nineteenth century, Giuseppe Pecchio, an Italian economist, patriot, and political refugee, who lived in England, went a little further. Indeed, he advanced the theory of the absolute supremacy of the economy over other manifestations of life in the political field and in literature. In a brief essay "On the extent to which scientific and literary production follow the general laws of economic production," Pecchio held that the quality and quantity of intellectual production does not depend on the form of the state, but on the law of supply and demand.[19]

THE CLASS STRUGGLE

All this research had given prominence, with many individual variations, to the importance of the economy in the historical development of the people and to the impact of economic factors on the mental habits of various classes and professions. Though implicitly admitting class antagonism, scholars had refrained from explicitly tracing its principles. Credit for first perceiving that in the struggle between two great economic classes lies the starting point and the "spiritus rector" of all human history belongs to the scion of one of the oldest families of the Neapolitan aristocracy, Gaetano

Filangieri. In effect, Filangieri said in 1780: "Observe the state of all nations, read the great book of societies; you will find them divided in two irreconcilable parties: the owners and the non-owners or hirelings." He then adds, "the proprietor will always seek to buy the hireling's labor at the lowest price possible, and the hireling will always seek to sell it to him at the highest price he can. In this negotiation, which of the two classes will succumb? This is evident: the more numerous. And which is the more numerous? To the common misfortune of Europe, by an enormous defect of legislation, the proprietor class is infinitely small in relation to that of the hirelings."[20]

Perhaps, by taking into consideration only the two extreme elements of society, Filangieri's idea seems to be excessively unilateral and schematic. Besides, it obviously exposes its flank to historical criticism as a theoretical generalization from a period and a country passing through conditions that were entirely peculiar, for that was precisely the case with the Neapolitan state at the end of the eighteenth century. It had no middle class and, except for the cultured bourgeoisie gathered in the capital, there was only the rich property owner on one side and the very poor rustic or unproductive "lazzarone" of the sub-proletariat on the other. The attempt at classification, however, was of some value, inasmuch as Filangieri introduced into the study of classes a scientific and clear criterion—that of property.

Class consciousness proper had its origin in the modern factories of Western Europe, especially in England and France. Work done in common in the very same shop generated a continuity of mechanical tasks that in the long run ended in the creation of some collective mental similarity.[21] To the community of environment and local surroundings was added the homogeneity of economic conditions. Therefore, the genesis of class consciousness in the new industrial proletariat is quite understandable.

At first it aroused in the workers the traces of a vague

"world cosmic sense" and an ethical cosmopolitanism. "Their country is the world," exclaimed Bulwer in 1833, entranced by the wage-workers of England whose hearts beat for foreign and subjugated peoples like the Polish, the Irish, and even the Negroes of Jamaica.[22] Thus the English proletariat gradually felt itself to be a people, so to speak, a human aggregation clearly distinct from the other classes of the population. One of the most acute observers of rising English industrialism, the German Engels, formulated in 1845 in definite terms the thesis that in every country the middle class had more ties of affinity with all the other middle classes of the world than with the workers who lived next door or even under the same roof. For, as Engels says, in the proletariat one encounters another jargon, other ideas, other sentiments, other customs and moral principles, another religion, and another political directive.[23]

Benjamin Disraeli, later Lord Beaconsfield, discussed this historical process in a novel with the characteristic title, *Sybil or the Two Nations*. There he repeated the idea that had caused him in his parliamentary discourse of 1840 to declare that the recognition of the proletariat's rights to its political emancipation and the betterment of its economic conditions was the only way to close the abyss that already separated the "two nations."

One can well understand how, things being as they were, public and scientific attention could no longer ignore a social class that had come to regard itself as a nation, apart from the rest of the people to whom it belonged. Consequently, in the period between 1830 and 1840 some writers devoted themselves to writing histories of the proletariat, among them a member of the French Parliament, Robert du Var[24] and the German, Bensen.[25] Meanwhile, however, the middle class, too, became the object of studies and historical research. In this field first honors go to the *History of the Third Estate* of Augustin Thierry. Adolphe Grainier de Cassagnac wrote in 1837 his *Historie des classes ouvrieres et des classes bourgeoi-*

ses. The author limits his scope to the era of the Renaissance. His work, however, is distinguished as an attempt to trace the history of the proletarian class and for its thesis that the true origins of present social strata are to be sought in ancient slavery, from which only three categories of persons succeeded in emancipating themselves: the learned, through their intelligence, the courtesans, through their beauty, and the bandits, through their strength.[26]

On one side, the studies were limited to a description of the history and the social conditions of certain classes, and, on the other side, the authors of some works, previously mentioned, were satisfied to make theoretical observations pertaining to an economic conception of history without connecting them with specific events. There was still a third kind of pre-Marxist works whose authors tried to apply the theory of historical materialism to the writing of history. Leaving aside the small posthumous work of Barnave, which in any case was published only in 1845, and the above-mentioned work of Engels, published in the same year, the *Histoire des dix ans* (1830–1840) by Louis Blanc, published in the years 1841–1844, is to be considered the first work of this kind. The example of Blanc's materialistic insight into the history of his time was followed a little later by Karl Wilhelm Nitzsch, then professor at the University of Koenigsburg, in his *History of the Gracchi*, published in 1847. This work molded the classical works of the contemporary small but daring group of German proponents of economic-political history.[27]

Also another well-known German historian, Georg Wilhelm von Raumer, recognized in 1854 in an incidental way the "necessity to understand that political events are the consequences of changes in the methods of production, in the ways of life, and in the kind of changes produced in the situation of the social classes by the metamorphosis of commerce and by the means of communication and transportation."[28] Raumer illustrated his thesis by saying that no power in the world is able to impede the abolition of servitude and the free distribution of landed property and of inheritance, so little are these measures necessary as means of production. Given the evident affinity of such a historical conception to Marxian historical materialism, Below is perfectly correct when he asserts that, in the period under examination, even so-called bourgeois science in Germany had shown, in its historical considerations, insight into economic influences. Historical materialism, therefore, has never been the monopoly of Marxism.

MARX AND PARETO

Nevertheless it is an indisputable merit of Marx and Engels to have been the first not only to erect as a system the particular part that the productive forces play in the historic process, but also to have assigned to them, with the creation of a new philosophy, their place in science.

They first did this in the *Communist Manifesto* in a rigid and vulnerable form, saying that the history of the world as it has developed up to the present time has been nothing but the history of class struggle, and that all phenomena, in whatever field of human activity encountered, would be understood as a "superstructure" built on an economic base. Later, however, the authors of historical materialism were forced to modify their theory considerably. As it appears from some letters written by Engels in 1890 and 1894, the parents of scientific socialism had by then defined their ideas in a new formula: to wit, that various political, juridical, and philosophical ideas, together with religious conceptions or dogmas, exercise a strong influence on the course of history. And in many cases these become even a preponderant force. Wrote Engels: "There are, therefore, innumerable dynamic tendencies, which cross each other reciprocally, an infinite series of parallelograms of the forces out of which, as a result, the historic happening springs."

And even later, in a letter of 1895, Engels ventured the opinion that "political evolution and its juridical, philosophical, literary, religious, and other facets rest, it is true, on the economic, but that each of them acts on the other and that all react together on the economic base."[29]

With this last reservation concerning the general application of the theory of historical materialism, Engels himself implicitly admitted the insufficiency of that single idea to explain the entire causality of historical events. For history is exceedingly complex and is inexpressible in a single formula. Vilfredo Pareto, not referring, it is true, to the qualifying letters, but only to the original sources, and taking therefore the historical materialism of the *Communist Manifesto* at its word, called it with elegant irony "the ideological superstructure of the real interests of the proletarian class."

Yet Pareto believed historical materialism was capable of rendering excellent services to science and to the proletariat itself. After all, according to Pareto, historical materialism clothes the elements of life with a criterion that is critical, scientific, and realistic to the point of re-entering the ambit of the great current of Darwinism. Marx, therefore, deserved credit for a "profoundly true idea and it is necessary to admire the energy and the strength of character that Marx has displayed in defending it from all and against all."[30] In the first book of his *Trattato di Sociologia Generale*, Pareto enunciated his thoughts in the following terms: "Historical materialism has been a notable scientific advance because it has helped to clarify the contingent character of certain phenomena, such as moral phenomena and religious phenomena, to which was given, and is given yet by many, an absolute character. Besides it certainly has an element of truth in insisting on the interdependence of economic phenomena and other social phenomena; the error stands in having changed this *interdependence* to a relationship of cause and effect."[31]

And in the second volume he adds, paraphrasing what has already been said, that "it is admitted that sentiments vary according to the kind of occupation. Along that path the theory of economic materialism, so-called, could be rejoined to my theory of the 'residues.' For the residues depend on economic conditions, and this is certainly true. But the error consists in wanting to separate economic conditions from other social phenomena, with which, instead, they are interdependent, and furthermore, in constructing a unique relation of causality instead of the many analogous relations that interlace with each other."[32]

In another note which Pareto directs to the Marxist concept of class struggle he perhaps disagrees less with Marx the sociologist than with Marx the economist, and also with the babel of the epigoni (for to distinguish himself from them Pareto used to say that he was not a Marxist). For Pareto indeed does not admit the absolute compactness of the two contending social classes. He observes that in the bosom of the very same proletariat a hidden struggle develops between organized and unorganized, class-conscious and non-class-conscious workers, while on the part of the middle class the small businessman asks to be protected from the big merchants and generally from the competition of more active men, to which is given the name, "unfair competition."[33]

In the complex of motives that induced Pareto to give his scientific and human esteem to the doctrine of historical materialism may be discerned a motive eminently energetic, one which considers historic materialism as an expression of a faith—for Pareto perceived in his basic residues certain dynamic forces necessary to the development of social struggles. Men are not impelled to action, he used to say, except by faith.[34]

Pareto does not want to contest the value of faith, opinions, and feelings to the development of politics and even individual human life. Rather, he thinks that faith and the struggle between the various faiths is an indispensable element to a sane and active life, alone able to prevent sloth and laziness. "Nonlogical actions" have their own profound reason for existence, which consists precisely in this: the ingenuous supposition that "man could do away entirely with religion and substitute for it simple scientific notions is an infantile error."[35]

Pareto likewise does not recognize one particular objection to historical materialism. With practically the same irony with which Marx had made ridiculous the idealistic socialism of Grun and Hess of his time, Pareto mocks the optimistic doctrine that does not want to admit the necessity of social struggle, and those who confuse the optimistic doctrine with the liberal one. To deny the existence of the rich and the poor, the proletarian and the middle class, alleging as a reason that social reality presents many intermediate shades, would be exactly like denying that there is high-priced and low-priced merchandise. "Because it is a fact that we insensibly go from one class of objects to the other, the existence of choices is not less real."[36]

Finally Pareto gives Marx the sociologist credit for having "explicitly affirmed principles which, until his time had been nothing but confused ideas, and for having made popular an historical theory, known until then to only a few scientists; and also for having discredited the unreal notion of those who want to explain facts with the ideas that men hold."[37]

The economic conception of history, the most genuine expression of which is precisely the historical materialism of Karl Marx, did not originally have any subversive flavor. With that conception, its supporters did nothing but ascertain some facts without occupying or preoccupying themselves with the results that such facts could bring. As Benedetto Croce well observes, historical materialism, deprived of the elements of finality or inevitable utopia which Marxist socialism wanted to confer upon it, cannot give any support to socialism or to any other practical way of life.[38] The economic conception of history is a doctrine that explains the reasons, the genesis, but does not help to illuminate socialism, which is a wishful vision of the future. It is silent on the outcome of the struggle it has traced through history.

The next pages aim to mark the boundaries within which historical materialism conforms to historical truth,[39] and above all to examine its place in political science.

NOTES

1. Ch. Rappoport, *La philosophie de l'histoire comme science de l'évolution*, Paris: Jacques, 1903, p. 81.
2. M. de La Fare, *Mémoires et réflexions sur les principaux Evènements du règne de Louis XIV et sur le Caractère de ceux qui y ont eu la principale part*, Nouv. ed., Amsterdam, 1782, p. 6ff.
3. Christian Garve, *Ueber den Charakter der Bauern und ihr Verhältnis gegen die Gutsherrn und gegen die Regierung*, Breslau: Korn, 1786, p. 5.
4. Adam Ferguson, *An Essay on the History of Civil Society*, new ed., Basle: Tourneisen, 1789, p. 279.
5. *Ibid.*, p. 227.
6. Diderot, *Encyclopédie ou Dictionnaire raisonné des Sciences*, etc., Paris, 1751, Vol. I (Leghorn ed., 1770, Vol. I, p. 682).
7. Adam Smith, *Inquiry on the Nature and Causes of the Wealth of Nations*, London: Dove, 1826, pp. 609–610.
8. Pietro Verri, *Meditazioni sull'economia politica*, Turin: Tip. Economica, 1852, p. 82.
9. Alberi, *Relazione degli ambasciatori veneti*, Serie II, Vol. I, p. 20.
10. J. R. MacCulloch, *The Principles of Political Economy*, Edinburgh: Black, 1843, 5th ed., 1864, p. 133.
11. Jules Michelet, *Le Peuple*, Geneva: Fallot, 1846, p. 33.
12. Adolphe Blanqui, *Précis élémentaire d'économie politique*, Paris: Mairet, 1843, p. 85.
13. Louis René Villermé, "Tableau de l'état physique et moral des ouvriers employés dans les manufactures de laine, de coton et de soie," in the *Mémoires de l'Academie des Sciences morales et politiques*, Nouv. série, Paris, 1838, Vol. II, p. 485.
14. Alexis de Tocqueville, *De la démocratie en Amérique*, Paris: Gosselin, 1840, Vol. II, 2, pp. 45–46, also my book, *Economia e Felicita*, Milan: Vallardi, 1919, pp. 28–44.
15. Ramazzini, *Saggio sopra la malattia degli artefici*, Venice: Antonelli, 1844, p. 22.
16. Cadet de Gassicourt, "Considérations statistiques sur le santé des ouvriers," in *Mémoires de la Société-Médicale d'émulation de Paris, 1816*, Paris: Migneret, 1817, p. 101.
17. Eduard Bernstein, "Ein französischer Parteiführer von 1799 als Vorläufer der materialistischen Geschichtsauffassung," *Dokumente des Sozialismus*, Vol. III (1903), p. 59.
18. Oeuvres de Barnave, Paris: M. Bérenger (de la Drôme), 1843. Cf. Jean Jaurès, *Histoire Socialiste, La Constituante*, Paris: Rouff, 1902.
19. Later published as an appendix to an interesting little volume on the history of finance and economy in the kingdom of Italy, *Saggio storico sull'amministrazione finanziera dell'Ex Regno d'Italia dal 1802 al 1814*, Turin: Tip. Ec., 1852, p. 133; cf. also Paolo Orano, *Il precursore italiano di Carlo Marx*, Rome: Voghera, 1899.
20. Gaetano Filangieri, *La scienza della legislazione*, 2nd ed., Leghorn: Masi, 1826, Vol. I, pp. 208–209.
21. This idea has been developed by myself on the basis of considerable historical documentation in the ninth volume of *Grundriss der Sozialoekonomik* by Max Weber (Michels, *Psychologie der antikapitalistischen Massen-Bewegungen*, pp. 241–360), Tübingen: Siebeck, 1925.

22. E. L. Bulwer, *England and the English*, Paris: Baudry, 1836, p. 65.
23. Friederich Engels, *Die Lage der arbeitenden Klassen in England*, 2nd ed., Stuttgart: Dietz, 1892, p. 127.
24. Robert du Var, *Histoire de la classe ouvrière depuis l'esclave jusqu'au prolétaire de nos jours*, Paris: Michel, 1845, 4 vols.
25. Heinrich Wilhelm Bensen, *Die Proletarier. Eine historische Denkschrift*, Stuttgart: Franck, 1847.
26. Adolphe Granier de Cassagnac, *Histoire des classes ouvrières et des classes bourgeoises* (1837), German edition, p. 327.
27. C. Jastrow, "Carl Wilhelm Nitzsch und die deutsche Wirtschafts- geschichte," in *Jahrbuch für Gesetzgebung, Verwaltung*, VIII (1881), pp. 873–897.
28. Georg von Below, *Die deutsche Geschichtsschreibung von den Befreiungs- kriegen bis zu unseren Tagen*, Leipzig: Meyer, 1916, pp. 125–126.
29. Eduard Bernstein, *Die Voraussetzungen des Sozialismus und die Aufgaben der Sozialdemokratie*, Stuttgart: Dietz, 1904, p. 7.
30. Vilfredo Pareto, *Sistemi socialisti*, Milan: Istituto Editoriale Scientifico, Vol. VI, pp. 220–221.
31. Vilfredo Pareto, *Trattato di sociologia generale*, Florence: Barbera, 1916, Vol. I, p. 426. (EDITOR'S NOTE: Translated into English as *The Mind and Society* by A. Bongiorno and A. Livingstone, New York: Harcourt, Brace and Co., 1935, 4 vols.)
32. Vol. II, pp. 276–277, also *Sistemi socialisti*, Vol. VI, p. 211. (EDITOR'S NOTE: The residues are non-logical impulses to act in a certain way; they may be compared roughly with predispositions and instincts. "Res- idues correspond to particular instincts in men, and for that reason they usually lack definite and precise quality. . . . The sentiments or in- stincts that correspond to residues, along with those that correspond with appetites and interests, etc., are the chief factors in determining the social equilibrium." Thus Pareto in his *Trattato*, loc. cit., section 870.)
33. *Sistemi socialisti*, VI, p. 267.
34. *Ibid.*, p. 264.
35. *Ibid.*, p. 233.
36. *Ibid.*, p. 236.
37. *Ibid.*, p. 219.
38. Benedetto Croce, *Materialismo storico ed Economia marxistica*, Milan- Palermo: Sandron, 1900, p. 31.
39. Georg Adler, *Die Grundlagen der Karl Marxschen Kritik der bestehenden Volkswirtschaft*, Tübingen: Laupp, 1887, p. 218. On the origins of his- torical materialism, see Walter Sulzbach, *Die Anfänge der materialistischen Geschichtsauffassung*, Karlsruhe: Braun, 1911, p. 82; F. Lenz, "Romantik und Marxismus über das Proletariertum," in *Vierteljahrsschrift für Sozial- und Wirtschaftsgeschichte*, 1913, p. 263; Emil Hammacher, *Das philo- sophisch-ökonomische System des Marxismus*, Leipzig: Duncker und Hum- blot, 1909, p. 54.

CHAPTER II

The Relation of Economic Events to Personality and Politics

ECONOMIC MAN

As WE have hitherto stated it, the theory of historical material-ism teaches us that a social group behaves to a high degree according to economic motivation. However, we have agreed with Pareto that it helps if one bears in mind that it is not possible to separate the economic from the social aspects of phenomena in the analysis of basic events, for the social inter-lace with the economic in a manner that is sometimes inex-tricable. The social group, furthermore, cannot always obey economic considerations if only because it lacks knowledge of what is expedient or economically useful. While it believes itself to be acting in agreement with its economic urges, it may be taking a course contrary to its economic interest. De Stefani rightly observes that "the revolutions that sub-stitute rulers, or limit their power, are always provoked by the critical attitude of a few apostles who do not always belong to the working class within which they operate, and who diffuse among the masses a faith in the possibility of satisfying, by some means and through some directive, a pre-existing but dormant need."[1]

In reference to "economic man" alone, even though he may in general feel himself impelled to achieve aims indicated by his economic interests, it can be said that his relations to the economy are often very complicated. For the economic way of life rarely admits distinct and clear separations from the other ways of human life. A German sociologist at the University of

Berlin, Georg Simmel, has advanced an interesting and note-worthy theory on the intersecting of various social circles in man. Simmel observes that each individual finds himself to be at the point of intersection of various social circles "the number of which is an indicator of the degree of his civiliza-tion." Each person's mental habit is determined by the various combinations of single groups, that is, by the various ways men have of associating with one another. Furthermore, each individual circle has a different hierarchical structure. There-fore man is forced to move at the same time upon different steps of the various hierarchical staircases. Simmel says: "Since there is no complete relation of interdependence between the various levels of the different positions simultaneously oc-cupied by the same person in his various groups, some strange combinations may appear. One such combination, for example, continuously emerges in the countries that have universal military training: that is, that a person who belongs to the highest intellectual class of his country may as a private have to obey orders given to him by a corporal who is socially and intellectually his inferior."[2]

Several other elements enter the picture to differentiate the circles of social solidarity—the principal profession, the sec-ondary, the favorite occupation, the often complex social posi-tion, belonging to a class, to a condition, to a party, to a progeny, to a region, to a nation, to a race, to a religion, to a family group, even membership in a sports association, a circle, a club, or one of the many other forms of social organization. All this exercises an influence over the individual's mentality and behavior, and causes in the same individual the formation of many competing affiliations, more or less heterogeneous, which struggle without truce to dominate his actions. It is pre-cisely this plurality of the individual's connections with un-limited and divergent social and economic circles that spurs man to perform acts the motives of which are as complex as his connections and therefore are only rarely traceable to a single cause. In such manner, even the acquisition of an honorary position of industrial leadership, or more generally the investment of capital, which seem to constitute the simplest economic actions imaginable, may be determined by sentiments of indulgence or weakness, by religious preconceptions, by love of fatherland, and by several other qualities or defects that have little or nothing in common with economics.

The stimulus of pure idea, ferocious adversary of pure economics, which induces the individual to disregard willingly his economic interests, often enters the contest. The individual, whether swayed by preconceptions, anger, fanaticism, or endowed with a strong character, can almost entirely break away from the bonds of his own profit; that is, he may pursue both in his personal and political life a line of conduct which is in incurable antithesis with it. As I have had occasion to confirm in several of my works,[3] there have been periods in the socialist movement during which the workers were led by enthusiasts and idealists from the upper classes, who spared no personal sacrifice to benefit the cause to which they had consecrated themselves. This was true above all when socialism was in its incipient state. In certain countries such as Russia and Italy, and also in France, men like Prince Kropotkin and Carlo Cafiero, owners of great estates, renounced their patrimony or spent their last cent for the advancement of their ideal, being content for themselves to live a modest life.

There are also peasants and manual workers who, though very poor, are greatly pleased with their lot and who partly because of inherent conservatism or because of intense gratitude and faithful devotion toward their master, would consider an injustice every law, even if enacted for their welfare, that would obstruct the full freedom of private property. We can see, even now, the most wretched of slave laborers working on the fields of the Prussian nobility's great estates humbly give his vote, at election time, to his Baron so that the Baron may keep his feudal flag waving high.

A typical example of ultimate superiority of the ideological factor over the material or economic factor is recorded in the history of the Civil War in the United States of America. There regiments recruited entirely from Negro slaves died in battle against the whites from the Northern states who had come to lead them toward their emancipation and break their chains of slavery.

Those considerations emphasize clearly that in real life the absolute abstraction of the economic man who is ruled over by economic principles does not exist. Man is not an economic counter. His life is a continuous struggle among economic necessities, a social stratum to which he belongs, and a conceded traditional sphere of interests and duties on one side. On the other side, impulses which stand, so to speak, above and perhaps beyond his material and social position may arouse in his heart passions likely to divert him from his natural economical course and to give his activity another direction, sometimes even utopian in nature.

Maffeo Pantaleoni, in one of his publications, appropriately exclaims: "I maintain that the recourse to factual data furnished to it by psychology should not be taken away from political economy, the contrary opinion of distinguished modern thinkers notwithstanding. I do not see what is to be gained by this renunciation; but I see what there is to lose. . . . It is a sterile aberration to want to formulate our analysis of human behavior as we unfortunately must formulate our analysis of the phenomena of dead nature. I cannot ask the clouds to tell me when and where they want to rain. I have to accumulate several thousands of observations to put together the necessary or sufficient conditions for their various ways of comportment. But men, when interrogated, answer."

Citing another fragment: "There is only one reason that would forbid us the use of psychological facts. That is: that though being facts, they could be sterile, or—what is really a case of extreme sterility—they could be extraneous to the argument. But it is well assured that those elementary data of psychology which serve the economist are so obvious that there are few others more reliable."[4]

We will illustrate this thesis, which we make our own, with only two examples taken from American and French economic history. Early in the last century, de Tocqueville, a traveler and an impartial and sagacious scholar, was amazed at how imbued the North Americans were with a craving for profits alone. The concept of work seemed devoid of judgment and vital sense. Even among the most wealthy, work was protracted to the point of fatigue, nervous exhaustion, and madness.[5] This is the prototype of the so-called pure economic man. As defined by a modern student of English economy, he is a person who works for profit and not to enjoy the profit of his work.[6] For such a type happiness consists in hoarding money, in the accumulation of wealth. Instead of collecting stamps or ancient coins he collects thousand-dollar bills.

Many, indeed, find in remunerative occupation the satisfaction for which they hoped. For many other Croesuses, on the contrary, money, from a chained and obedient slave, transmutes itself into an absolute master, which exploits and crushes them. In such a case, the work accomplished to obtain wealth, rather than being a bearer of happiness, becomes a mania, a fixed idea, an obsession, an incubus, that imperiously demands that everything of value be immolated to it, including the tranquility of his mind and sexual love. The life of such men is so morbidly strained by a financial iron will that business cares completely absorb them. There is no time, even among single men, for love affairs; yet, as they have remained asexual for craze of money, so they continue, even after marriage, to prefer money to women, and if they succeed in becoming wealthy, they force their wives to lead a life of idle abandonment, with its inseparable companion, flirtation. The wives, looked upon aloofly by husbands who have grown old in turbulent and sordid work, are thrown into the arms of the first dandy who knows how to entice and deceive them. Meanwhile, the moneyed ones during natural life remain nailed to the desk of their offices, or, foolish and restless as the proverbial wandering Jew, run about the halls and corridors of the Stock Exchange. They will have no peace until they leave this world.

France, which enjoys a high level of civilization and also has a low birth rate, and to a lesser extent other European countries have developed a different mentality, which belongs to those who live on rentals or fixed income. The "rentier" is the man who has created for himself a modest economic ideal, an earthly and attainable ideal. After having put away a small capital, the rentier changes his ways of life. He will spend his remaining days either pleasurably absorbed by artistic and political interests, or devoted to his children, in education, or even, after the manner of Hindu fakirs, in gazing at his umbilicus. At all events, he is absorbed in non-economic actions or contemplation. To this category of rentiers we will add another, those who set an age limit to their activity; they will quit at forty or at forty-five years of age, living well or badly on the patrimony scraped together up to that time or, if they have been employed, on the pension due to them. Both of these types coincide in that they have firmly decided not to exploit their working strength to the limit of exhaustion. Economically speaking, they do not give to themselves and their country the productivity that they could give; they take care of themselves. The cause of this mentality is found in the relative conception that those types have of the happiness potentiality of wealth. According to the rentiers, wealth is not an object in itself; evidently they refuse to believe in the boundless capacity of economic possessions to provide human happiness.

Tendencies of this sort occurred at the beginning of American industrialism.[7] In German Austria, mostly among the Hebrew element, who are anything but financially indolent and apathetic, a great number prefer the tranquil enjoyment of their acquired wealth to the feverish quest for riches. But the most typical country for the "living on one's income" mentality remains always France; therefore, we are not wrong in classifying it as "the French type." So it is that among some French entrepeneurs the ideal of retiring from business at a flourishing age is quite strong. Their adversaries often reproach them for it.[8] The French themselves, instead, value such a mentality as an indication of civil progress. Edmond About in his book, *Le Progres*, says: "Here a merchant does not have to vegetate forty years behind a counter to gather a small pension: seven or eight hours a day, ten or twelve years of work suffice to build up an honest capital resource."[9]

It is true, however, that post-war complications, the destruction of many patrimonies, and the necessity of "renouveau," have brought even in France a large decrease of the type described.

Another disturbing phenomenon for the "economic man" arises from his own physical nature. Corrado Gini, in fact, on the basis of a number of statistical and other considerations on human procreation, exclaims "how far from the truth is the hypothesis of 'economic man,' since if man really would act as an economic man, that is, on the basis of a calculated profit, and not dominated by impulses, the birthrate would be enormously reduced."[10] It is clear then that the term "economic man," so often used, is not applicable except in the Paretian sense. That is, it may be used precisely "to dissever and study separately from the rest only those actions of a man which are related to economics, constructing for the rest of his actions, according to the motives which determine them, other concepts such as the 'ethical man,' 'the religious man,' etc."[11]

However, those who would reproach the economist because his object of study is only the "economic man," in the sense above indicated, would commit the same error as those who would reproach an individual, desirous of establishing a theory of chess, for not wanting to concern himself with the culinary art. A word of caution, nevertheless: in going from the abstract to the concrete, naturally it is obligatory to reunite again the parts that have been separated in order to study them. Pareto in his *Manuel* says: "Science is essentially analytical; practice, on the contrary, is essentially synthetic."[12] This point of view, logically unexceptionable, has been thoroughly explained by Pantaleoni. If it is true that it is possible to segregate, always for scientific purposes, the zones in which the economic, the ethical, the religious, and other types of men move, yet these zones also vary greatly not only in the course of history, but also from individual to individual, according to the more or less of the "ethical" and the "religious" that the "economic man" has in himself, and according to the kind of ethical man and religious man that enter the picture.[13]

But, as we have said, man in his economic actions is at the mercy not only of the physical influence of various extra-economic coefficients. There is more to it. There is an absence of stability in the economic factor. There are several categories of economic man. Let us point out the immense multitude of persons whose economic status is not fixable except statically or temporarily. Such is the case, for example, with the Emilian sharecropper or the small landowner of Lombardy who, during the period of grape gathering, must hire a few workers to help with the dispatch of rural work. Yet in the other seasons of the year their small farms do not produce enough to support them. So they must send their children and their wives to Novara for the rice-husking period.[14]

Francesco Pulle relates the following on the "neutral" status of the peasants of upper Lombardy (province of Como): "Here is the individualized family that comes apart: the woman, the old people, the children stay at home and represent the condition of cultivators-proprietors; the husband and the children who are past twelve years of age are for eight months in the condition of workers out of town and only for four months in the condition of proprietors at home. Therefore, the image of the small proprietor that could be separated from the other image of the peasant and worker is not present; they combine the features of the peasant and the industrial worker."[15] These men are masters or hirelings

according to the season. Their interest and economic mentality will periodically change with the changing of their
social positions and according to the different periods of the
year.

Such is the case, also, with the daughters of landowners
or the hotel owners of Switzerland who, in order to learn
housekeeping or hotel service and table waiting, enter the
homes of the elite, or go through the season as so-called
"Saaltochter" in some high-class hotel. For the persons in
this group, the period of economic dependency is only an
intermediary position, of temporary obligation and transient
passage. No repercussion arises from this temporary social
condition on their total psychology; therefore they do not
feel they belong to any economic or political class organization.

Apart from the dualisms that issue from periodicity in the
exercise of certain trades, there are also others that arise
from the absolute simultaneity of more than one economic
condition. The result is neither contrary nor contradictory.
How many house owners are there who live voluntarily or
perforce in hotels not their own, who must at the same time
safeguard the interests of the renting tenant and of the proprietor? And how many workers are there who live not only
by the earnings of their labor, but enjoy also a small revenue,
obtained by them from a small rural property or joint-prop-
erty, or from small savings invested in a savings bank, or,
as it happens in some regions of England, from having been
able to acquire a share on margin?[16] In such a case they are
both the "exploited," inasmuch as the system subtracts day
by day a part of the work done by them, the so-called plus-
value, whose sum constitutes the capitalistic profit in the
most strict sense of the word, and the "exploiters," inasmuch
as they themselves also live by the fruit of somebody else's
labor. It must be admitted that the so-called right to the
integral product of his own labor is in such a case of difficult
application.

According to this very complicated interlacing of social relationships, the definite attitudes of man to economic problems arise from the major or minor economic weights attributed from time to time to each of the opposite functions exercised by him. But his attitude can derive also from an individual extra-economic sentiment of his own, to wit, his answer to the question: Which of my dissimilar economic functions is dearer to me?

ECONOMICS AND THE SOCIOLOGY OF RELIGION

We will treat, briefly, some of the causal connections between economics and religion.

A Protestant minister has maintained that the machine is a purely "Protestant" implement.[17] In the sociology of religion, others have presented Protestantism as the creed of the wealthy. Max Weber, who is to be considered the most authoritative among the students of the connections between religious and economic phenomena, is in the right when he warns against the tendency to lower religious movements to the level of simple reflexes or consequences of economic processes. Weber opportunely observes that the religious schism of the sixteenth century divided the populations affected by it in a vertical sense, not earning the sympathy of some particular stratum in preference to some other, but that of single individuals belonging to very dissimilar strata. Only later, certainly in part for economic reasons, did a positive relationship between confessional divisions and class differentiation appear here and there.[18] It so appears that since its inception really some of the richest regions have been converted to Protestantism, and particularly many of the most opulent cities. The effects of this phenomenon have not disappeared with the passing of time.

In a large portion of the European countries, as, for example, in Germany, France, Switzerland, Holland, and, also in our Piedmont even now, the percentage of wealth is higher in the Protestant part of the population than that of the Catholics. According to Weber, the obvious reasons of a historic and economic nature are not sufficient to explain the actual flourishing prosperity of all the Protestant nations. Another concurring essential factor is the existence in Protestantism of a marked psychological predisposition to the pervading influence of modern capitalism, which spurs the Protestant populations to direct their activity preferably toward professions promising sumptuous economical earnings.

The causes for the development of a capitalistic attitude among Protestants would be found in the specific direction given in their families to the children's education. According to the precepts of the Protestant religion and more so, indeed, of its "Puritan" subspecies, the first virtue of each good Christian consists in the scrupulous accomplishment of his own duties, and above all, his professional duties. In the second place, in comparison with Catholicism, which creates, in its adepts, a gayer, happier, more carefree, and more "artistic" temperament, Protestantism perhaps gives a major impulse to the spirit of individual initiative, for the reason that it confers on the same individual all the direct and immediate responsibility before God, not admitting any intercession whatever, neither by the Saints nor by altruistic prayers.

There is more: Catholicism recommends good works to facilitate the believer's entry into paradise; Protestantism recommends not only absolute rectitude in one's relations with his fellowman, but also the most strict observance of all contractual obligations assumed with him, so as to acquire the favor of public opinion that is believed necessary for the success of a business or a liberal profession. Many of the most prosperous Protestant sects in the Anglo-Saxon countries deny *a priori* that divine grace is susceptible of being *acquired* by man, it being reserved to those among the faithful who have been *predestined* to it.

From this complex of precepts and teaching would issue, in the Protestant populations, an individualistic, vigorous, hard-working, and, under some conditions, fatalistic mentality, very much intent on taking care of its own profit (provided it is honest), but given also to running the risks that business life brings with it. From the historical and sociological research of Weber, contained in a great book,[19] one may deduce the thesis that it is not the economy that makes its imprint on the religious sentiment, but rather that the type of mentality created by the religious discipline develops in its followers the above-mentioned economic attitudes.

Others see the origins of capitalism in the Hebraic religion. Werner Sombart, convinced of the importance that religious doctrines have for the economic spirit of their addicts, has in his turn exhaustively demonstrated what and how much influence the precepts of the Hebraic faith exert in the development of the capitalistic instinct of the people, in perfect contrast to the doctrine of historical materialism, considered to be "the embodiment of the capitalistic-mercantile spirit."[20]

As for economic power, whether of the Protestants or of the Jews, the centuries have furnished abundant proof. Thus, from the point of view of economic history we may associate the economic decadence of Spain with the expulsion of the Jews, and the flourishing of Northern Holland, especially Amsterdam, with the fact that the major portion of those Jews emigrated to precisely those regions (1492, 1609–11). The development of Amsterdam dates truly, apart from the devastation of Antwerp by the Spaniards and the immigration of the Flemish (1579–1586), from the influx of five thousand Jews from the Iberian Peninsula.

Similarly the revocation of the Edict of Nantes—what need be said of Nimes!—by Louis XIV in the year 1685 and the emigration during the three years following, of more than fifty thousand Protestant families (later on the exodus was calculated to be four hundred thousand persons or more) impoverished France in the same manner that it enriched, from the point of view of commerce and industries, the bordering countries, except Spain. Voltaire very justly says of these refugees: "They carried to foreigners the arts, manufacturing, and riches. Almost all of Northern Germany, a country still wild and barren of industries, took on a new face as a result of the multitude of refugees. They peopled entire cities. Cloth, lace, hats, and stockings, which one used to buy from France, were made by them. A whole district of London was peopled by French silk workers; others carried there the highly skilled art of glass manufacture which was thus lost to France."[21]

The refugees brought to Zurich, Switzerland, the art of silk weaving and to Geneva that of watchmaking; it was they who established the cultivation and manufacturing of tobacco in Prussia. The Huguenots are the real makers of modern Germany. Ettore Rota rightly said: "They rid the Prussian state of all the miasma from the swamps that infected even the capital of the Mark; from the microbes of ignorance and superstition that were keeping the common people in a state of misery. They transformed the sands of Brandenburg into gardens, the slums of Berlin into palaces; they taught the principles of good government; they introduced in Prussia the industries of Paris; they educated the princes; they civilized the court and the clergy; they founded schools, colleges, academies of all sorts."[22]

Both cases, that of the Spanish Jews as that of the French Huguenots, represent historical events of the highest importance, because, although arising from entirely different presuppositions, they caused profound changes in the economic field. Here we see, indeed, not the ideological superstructure on the economic substructure, but *vice versa* an economic superstructure on a psychological-ideological base that is rather distinctly political and religious. Religious intolerance was the occasional cause for the industrially or commercially most productive part of certain populations to abandon the country, transferring their genius, their activity, and their industriousness elsewhere. Bourbon France forced the inhabitants of the richest and most developed provinces, especially those from the south, to leave the country. Hapsburg Spain persecuted the Jews and their baptized descendants (Marrani). And this was a race that, wherever given refuge and liberty of movement from its enforced peregrinations, made trade and commerce flourish. And whenever expelled, it left behind stagnation and economic ruin. It is clear that, without these extra-economic phenomena, on one side Protestant Germany and on the other side Holland could not have acquired economic prosperity or only very much later and more slowly.

The pattern of transplantation of industry from one country to another owing to such heavy migration caused by political persecutions does not reveal some impulsive, occult force of an economic nature. To my knowledge, there has not been up to the present time any follower, no matter how fanatic, of historic materialism, who would have dared attempt to place the Hebraic emigration from Spain and the exodus of the Huguenots from France as links in the chain of historical phenomena to be considered materialistically, in the Marxist sense of the word. At the present state of historical research, therefore, we are faced with the fact that, in economics, changes determined by political-religious motives are possible.

Even psychological suggestion or auto-suggestion serves to produce most grave effects on an economy, modifying its normal course. Here is an example, little known but suggestive and not wanting in historical interest. In 1576 there died at the early age of twenty-five King Sebastian of Portugal, in the battle of Alcazar against the Moors. His death marked the beginning of a long series of inauspicious years for Portugal. It lost its national independence and had to suffer Spanish domination, during which its economic interests were neglected and seriously impaired. But the people obstinately refused to believe the most reliable news of the disappearance of its prince and waited patiently for the return of King Sebastian, which would be the divine signal for the resumption of the ancient glory and prosperity of Portugal. This popular hope, which soon assumed superstitious form, quickly introduced itself also into the very economic life of the country.

In fact, in about the year 1660, that is to say, more than a century after the death of the unhappy monarch, it was a common occurrence in Portugal to lend money and sell merchandise on credit, with the sole obligation on the debtor to pay back double the value of the loan upon the King's return.[23] The myth generated such usages as to cause in the Portuguese economy particular redistributions of wealth of formidable proportions and even provoked a financial crisis.

POLITICAL ECONOMY AND NATIONAL POLITICS

Effects of Political Measures on Economic Life. The institution of far-reaching political measures can, according to the circumstances, decidedly favor or ruin an economy in its very foundations. We have already cited two examples of this, taken from the history of France and of Spain. As a matter of principle, it is not right to ignore the question whether a certain political measure that has provoked some economic change has not been determined at bottom in its turn by economic causes. Nevertheless the answer to this interjection will frequently be negative. Nor would it be hard to give the answer in an appropriate work of several volumes, replete with proof taken from the life of all times and all peoples. Permit us, however, to extract from the mass of evidence one example only.

The Continental Blockade was invoked by Napoleon I for essentially political purposes, with the object of forcing England to cease making war against France and to renounce her intervention in continental affairs. In spite of its brief duration and its imperfect administration, the measure produced on England's commerce and industries, as on the economic development of the countries under the influence of Napoleon, some formidable effects. The blockade overturned all the old connections between importation and exportation, and substituted others in their place, soon giving life to new branches of industry. Italy in the eighteenth century had been flooded with pottery by England. After the royal decree forbidding its importation, factories sprang up all over the country: at Como, Milan, Treviso, Pavia, Vicenza, and Bologna.

On the other side of the ledger, the textile and ribbon and veil industries, that were flourishing especially at Bologna, and the prosperity of which depended to a great deal on heavy exports to England, collapsed. Similarly, England compensated for the blocked importation of Italian veils by building new plants for their production. The inroads of the Continental Blockade on the structure of Italian industry and commerce can be summarized in the words of the forementioned contemporary economist, Giuseppe Pecchio: "All industries depending on internal consumption registered an uncommon boom, while those industries which manufactured articles for exportation, instead, decayed abjectly."[24]

The same thing happened in Saxony, in the Rhenish Provinces and in other parts of continental Europe. In Saxony the textile industry which, owing to tremendous British competition was dying away, suddenly, after the formation of the Continental Blockade, rose to unprecedented productivity."[25]

In the Rhineland, commerce in trans-shipments and in produce coming from English colonies, diminished enormously. Not even contraband, a flourishing enterprise of vast dimensions, sometimes engaged in even by the patricians of Cologne, could, as things were, bring any change in the situation. In a vain attempt to eradicate contraband, Napoleon finally resorted to violence, burning all English merchandise found on the continent. Since the most flourishing contraband could never have replaced regular or regulated commerce, on the left bank of the Rhine under the fatherly protection of the French government arose new and very important kinds of industry. For example, to substitute for cane sugar, large factories to manufacture beet sugar were built;[26] thus, in general, the present flourishing sugar industry of the continent owes its origin to the political measures taken by France in the struggle against England. So sprang up also, in the Rhenish towns, the important spinning and textile industries, believed to be capable of rendering English cloth superfluous.[27] In 1813 there were in the city of Cologne not less than twenty-three cotton manufacturing establishments.[28] It can be said that the Continental Blockade changed the economic nature of the Rhenish capital. At the time of the French entry, although for a long period business had been poor and decadent, the city had a distinctly commercial character; fifteen years of French occupation and Napoleonic politics transformed it into a prosperous industrial city.

Economic Effects of War and Change in the State. Not only the tariff system in its many forms and historical examples, but also the outcome of battles can, in some cases, create or destroy entire industries. The transfer of a province from one state to another often produces a complete disruption of its industrial and commercial relations. This upset is caused by changes in the market, provoked as it is by the shift of the customs frontiers that comes with the change of dominion. This appears clear, for example, when one considers the political-commercial consequences brought forth in 1815 by the separation of the left bank of the Rhine from France. For the inhabitants of that region it meant, above all, the loss of the French market, and the outbreak of a new tariff war with Holland, which with her import and export duty, soon almost completely paralyzed inland navigation. In the year 1822 some merchants of Cologne found themselves compelled to dump into the sea, before entering Dutch territorial waters, a cargo of 300 tons of herrings coming from Sweden, the transit duty demanded by the Dutch government being so high that the fish could not have been sold in Cologne.[29]

But what acted more perniciously on the economy of Cologne was the suppression, following the annexation of the Rhenish provinces to Prussia, of the prohibitive French customs duties, which had been established to protect the local young industry. Like the outbreak of a disastrous flood, after the restoration of free trade, promised by Prussia to England in return for loans granted by it to finance the wars against Napoleon, English competition after a brief contest dealt a mortal blow to the young cotton industry and even to sugar production in Cologne. The same fate awaited the silk industry.[30] Later, however, the direct conjunction of the city with the sea through the construction of a railroad branch to Antwerp finally rendered Cologne independent of the river transportation of the Rhine and of the Dutch who controlled the estuary of the river. This and other devices were successful in pushing the commerce and industry of the city, almost obliterated by the Congress of Vienna's order to incorporate with Prussia, toward a new, rather grandiose prosperity. With all that, a portion of Rhenish industry created by Napoleon could never rise again.

Another typical example for the thesis that the transfer of a country from the dominion of one state to that of another, in consequence of political events, can bring grave economic crises, comes to us from the history of Alsace-Lorraine before and after 1870. Following the German conquest and occupation, the Alsatian textile industry lost the French market and it was only through a very hard struggle that it succeeded in finding an equivalent outlet in the German Empire. This substitution, however, could not be accomplished without leaving profound traces in the structure of Alsatian economy and without producing important ch₁nges in its industries. Thus, after the annexation, the cotton industry suffered a general reduction, while the woolen industry, after a brief pause, went forward to a splendid development. Alsace-Lorraine was returned to French rule after the World War, and the textile industry, created by the French, and never having strayed from its traditions, did not delay its reorientation toward France.

Such was not the case with the steel industry of Lorraine, which was of German creation, intimately interlaced as it were, in its finances, supplies, and commercial outlets with the Rhenish-Westphalian coal fields. The crisis which this most important industry, until lately the pride and support of vast regions of Lorraine, is presently going through, has been the object of a comprehensive and accurate study by Professor Henry Laufenburger of Strasbourg University. He proclaimed the absolute necessity for the steel industry of Lorraine to maintain, through special treaties between the two governments, financial ties with the economic interests, now extraterritorial, of the Rhenish-Westphalian coal regions. He expresses also the hope that allowing the substitution of the German steel market for that of the French could help to fill the very great need of French agriculture for farm implements.[31]

Examining, in the light of the facts, the modern history of peoples and of states we discover without difficulty the coexistence of two laws, or call them tendencies if you will, dissimilar and irreconcilable by their nature. We allude to the tendency of economic unification and to that of national unification. The first shows the necessity of modern people to unite for the creation of ever greater economic spheres, comprehensive and homogeneous, constituting extensive zones of production and great commercial enterprise. Such are territories that, according to the rule of natural economical differentiation, embrace agrarian and industrial zones, banking centers, and maritime ports, which thus form or tend to form a real "autarchy."

But another "law" still exercises control over modern history, that of national unification. This law tends to unite the two ideas of state and nation and to give life to national states. At its base is the application, more or less rigid it is understood, of the principle of nationality. It contributes *ipso facto* to the growth of new states, often very small, and thus, sometimes, it moves in antithesis to the economic phenomenon. For on its behalf many great economic complexes of long standing and established function are broken. There is no one now who does not see that after the World War the treaties of Versailles and Trianon, in the collision of these two tendencies, gave preference most of the time to the principle of nationality, openly sacrificing, when a choice was needed, the economic interests to the interests of nations or peoples.

Nor does the economist have the right, in our opinion, to curse this new idealistic ray that illuminates, or at least intends to illuminate the world, unless he ingenuously believes that the history of humanity is nothing but the everlasting search for immediately useful materials. The most obvious example of the above-mentioned preference given to the national factor is the way Austria was treated. Even those who hold untenable the thesis of the Austrian economists and their sympathizers, who proclaim that the origin of the defunct Austro-Hungarian Empire should be sought in the natural community of economic interests of the Danubian countries, cannot doubt that the very existence, political and national and lasting over several centuries, of an Austria-Hungary, was instrumental in creating a vast legal and economic unity, a vast internal market. This was destroyed by the peace treaty, which broke to pieces the economic unity in favor of the various national and ethnic entities. We repeat that, nevertheless, we may be very happy that this solution of such an intricate problem is perhaps the least evil one.

On the other hand, we should understand that from the exclusively economic viewpoint such *emiettement* of the ancient unity is a backward step on the road toward economic liberalism. As a result of it, in the first place, industrial production suffered. For it had been characterized at the time of the Hapsburg empire by a precise and minute division of labor between the various regions, which were now separated by political and custom frontiers. Thus, to take the clothing industry, what is now Czechoslovakia did 90 per cent of the cloth weaving, while 30 per cent of the manufacturing was produced by the city of Vienna alone.

In general it could be said that, except for the more complex banking business in which for traditional and geographical reasons Vienna had always been supreme, the present economic life of Austria depends entirely on the consent of other states, which were then part of its territory but are now free and independent. Such are Czechoslovakia and Hungary. Given this situation, it is not surprising that among men of affairs and Austrian economists a new movement has appeared, which declares that the only salvation of the tangled economic situation of the countries born of the Austrian monarchy would consist at a minimum in the formation of a customs union.[32] The thesis is difficult to apply nor apparently could it be effective without the definite and deliberate good will of Italy, whose national interests insistently demanded the blocking of a customs union that would be used by advocates as a beginning or pretext for the restoration, be it even under a different form, of the monstrous Danubian empire. But, for the rest, the above-mentioned thesis is still worthy of discussion.

Economic Strength and Political Power. One of the favorite themes of the Venetian writers and their sympathizers of the fifteenth and sixteenth centuries was to compare Venice and Rome. They maintained that Venice, from its very beginning a maritime nation, did not follow the sea to subjugate other states, but, so far as the times and conditions allowed, to seek trade and commercial profit. Peace and free trade with everyone were favored. But Rome, on the other hand, was primarily bellicose and martial.[33] Therefore the Romans after some time declined, while the life of Venice seemed to her sons to be eternal, and indeed it was prosperous for many centuries. Certainly Huet could not but admit that the Romans looked at navigation mostly from a military standpoint.[34] In another passage of his celebrated study, Huet declared that the Romans, following in this respect the example of their neighbors, wisely did not ignore the fact that commerce was the surest means to acquire the wealth essential to their other designs.[35]

Mengotti, however, observed that it was well to distinguish between the petty traffic found in any nation, even the poorest and most uncultured, and that larger commerce, whose per-

vading influence spreads through the whole nation, imparts
life to industry, the arts, and navigation, which is in turn ani-
mated by it, and enriches the empire, rendering it flourishing
and respectable. He adds that it is exactly this kind of commerce that the Romans never knew.[86] Mengotti then pursued
his criticism to the point of saying that the Romans, poor and
military, had neither genius, solicitude, nor knowledge of
economic affairs. From the first Punic War to the battle of
Actium (31 B.C.) they thought only of enriching themselves
by booty from other nations. He thought one must concur
with the opinion of Raynal, expressed in his *Histoire Philosophique et Politique*, that the Romans pursued no commerce
beyond that of transporting to Italy the wealth of Africa,
Asia, and the rest of the conquered world.[87] Modern historical criticism could not fail to recognize the importance and
pertinence of these researches. The present government of
Rome seems to realize this, since it is making strong attempts
to give to the city an industrial and commercial aspect, while
yet preserving intact its eternal artistic grandeur and natural
charm.

Only at one point is Mengotti wrong, but the error is of
momentous import. This is when he, able physiocrat that
he was, demanded: "Which empire is more stable, that of
force or that of industry?"[88] The question here poses a false
dilemma; for the more stable empire is not indeed that of
force separated from industry, nor that of industry free from
force and lacking government protection, but the more stable
empire appears to be that in which industry and force (and
many other factors also) alternately pervade and attend one
another.

Such a controversy logically leads us to another that is analogous: Does a particular economy presuppose a certain form
of government? A legal study cannot prove by valid historical
argument that a certain form of government would be the
essential "superstructure" of observed and determined economic and productive relationships. Despotism, for example,

we find blooming in the tyrannies that ruled several cities of Magna Graecia, in the Roman empire, in many feudal states of the Middle Ages, in the French empire, and among the pastoral Kafirs, and therefore, may be based on many kinds of economy.[39]

The political life of a nation often is far from being an adequate expression of the prevalent form of its economic life. A most persuasive example is found in the surprising paradox that dominated the life of prewar Germany. Germany, economically considered, appeared modern to us. In fact, as a country of the industrial-capitalistic type, the percentage of its inhabitants employed in industry and commerce was in 1882 already considerably higher than the percentage of those engaged in agriculture (45.5 against 41.4) and this ratio was growing higher each year in the direction of a greater industrial population. A few years later, in 1895, 50.6 per cent of the population was engaged in commerce and industry, while no more than 34.4 per cent was occupied in agriculture. However, for all that concerned the form of government, the spirit of its political organization, usages, and customs, Germany continued to appear highly feudal and aristocratic. To the distinctly industrial-capitalistic tenor of the economy was related, then, an atavistic precapitalistic form of government.[40]

In Prussia, more than in any other state of Germany, the so-called "political class" was made up of "Junkers" and government functionaries. Even to the sons of the great industrialists the regiments considered most aristocratic and the highest political ranks remained closed. Traces of ancient feudal rule persisted even in the juridical order: some of the labor laws were not extended to workers in the fields; to them the rights of organization and strike were denied and they were still subjected to the masters' jurisdiction in a number of ways. The real estate proprietors, driven back economically to the second line, showed themselves more capable of political resistance against the attack of the labor movement and against its influence on the state than the bourgeoisie, who were economically more powerful in the cities.

The economic life of modern France also shows a structure distinctly capitalistic, although not as much as that of Germany does. The productive classes, though economically very active, almost abandon the control of government to the intellectual classes, which are fossilized in the democratic ideas of years gone by and incapable of comprehending the needs of modern production. Control goes to the intellectuals, harshly referred to as prostitutes by Berth, a disciple of Sorel, because they give themselves indeterminately to all parties, whose economic interests they, however, do not make their own and cannot support.[41]

Erwin Szabo, a cultured Hungarian Marxist, justly observes, therefore, that the same economic base admits, in the various countries, according to the kind of interdependent relations existing among the surviving forces of past economies and old traditions, the most dissimilar social and political structures.

But if the economic base does not determine in itself the political and social directives of the nation, one may raise the question if, instead, the political form of the state determines the course of economic policy.

Gaetano Mosca, who is to be considered without doubt as one of the most profound contemporary sociologists,[42] declared once: "If democratic doctrines, and above all the liberal ones, have not been able to realize a government by majority they, however, have made it possible, in Western Europe and North America, over many generations, to have a period of economic prosperity, established justice, and relative social peace, which the other political forms never have attained."[43] This statement contains two affirmations—with the first of them (that denies the possibility of a majority government), I perfectly agree. Achille Loria reproaches me for not considering in my books on the subject, especially my *Sociologia del Partito Politico nella Democrazia Moderna*, that the elector always has the power to take away the mandate given the elected. He goes so far as to say that the "temporariness and consequent revocability of the political mandate actually succeed in maintaining the imperative mandate, as they impose on elected officials a directive of conduct which alone can assure their re-election."[44] Here he certainly sets himself in opposition not only to the theories accepted by professors of constitutional law (which perhaps would not be a capital sin), but also to the clearest laws of collective psychology. For he seems to attribute to the electorate some faculty of control and intrinsic autonomy that surely it does not possess.

But Mosca's statement contains also in embryo another thesis, more worthy of discussion. It cannot be denied that in England economy and democracy are synonymous. But the question arises whether such coincidence is inevitable or if it is characteristic of the sociological laws in force in all countries and at all times. We will examine briefly this point of doctrine in the light of history.

The historian cannot but remain impressed by the significant fact that the epoch of absolute monarchy was signalled in the field of political economy by the theory called mercantilism. In the development of commerce and industry was perceived to be the very pivot of economic progress and national "happiness." The first duty of sovereigns was to occupy themselves continuously with the economic conditions of their country. So it is stipulated, as Genovesi sternly declares, that commerce increases the power of monarchs and peoples; the sinews of power are the basic and characteristic riches that come from commerce.[45]

As for England in particular, it is well not to forget that before she became the birthplace of free trade, she had been the parent of applied protectionism and that to this, and not to the other, does she owe the first and strongest root of her economic prosperity, codified in the Navigation Acts. Even the very founder of the school of free trade, Adam Smith, subjects a difficult problem not only to the visible tool of economic theory, but also to that of the national interest, for "defense is of much more importance than opulence."[46] It appears from the descriptions of English economy, found in Antonio Zanon's well-known *Letters on Agriculture, Art and Commerce*[47] the Stuarts and Cromwell (who, if he was a republican and a revolutionary, was not really a democrat, and not even a liberal) vied eagerly with one another to promote England's economic greatness. In his chapter on the colonial policies of his time, Adam Smith wrote that the English colonies, despite their inherent inferiority regarding the natural fertility of the soil, presented a productivity greater than either the Spanish or Portuguese colonies, and he thought he could explain this enigma by the political and economic institutions of England, which were more favorable to improvement and cultivation of the land than those of Spain and even those of France.

However, we will observe that the subject of inquiry was not the difference in the form of the state, but only in economic "institutions," for example, hereditary rights, land taxes threatening with expropriation the inept agriculturist. In short, they were institutions that were perhaps dressed up in democratic character at the time of Smith, but they are now part of the juridical outfitting of every modern state. Even if it could be affirmed that the welfare of the English colonies depended, at least in part, on the more democratic policies of England of those days in comparison with other European states, today such a judgment is deprived of value as an exaggeration of a historical fact. For the modern state, even if it has remained or again become autocratic, has absorbed, in scarcely recognizable ways, some elements logically and historically of democratic origin.[48]

The bases of the flourishing French economy, it appears to me, were not democratic either. Modern French economy goes back in many ways to Colbertism, which was awkwardly counterfeited by its foreign imitators, who transformed it into a shirt of Nessus. Mengotti attacked its remains that were about to be swept away by the French Revolution, at a time when it already had for various reasons outlived itself. Yet now one cannot read Clement's collection of the detailed operations of the great minister of Louis XIV without experiencing a feeling of admiration for that great creator of French industry and commerce.

Another pioneer of the prosperous French economy was Napoleon, who himself cannot but be considered politically as a man of the democratic movement. Napoleon, advised by Chaptal and other experts, was also an able commercial organizer in his own right. He founded that powerful and, if well-managed, profitable institution that is the Chamber of Commerce. For the common people, who form their opinion of historical events only by their appearance—which historically are called "successes"—the Continental Blockade, undertaken by the great Corsican to destroy English commerce by suppressing the sale of English or Anglo-colonial merchandise in Europe, is now reputed to have been a foolish enterprise. We are not so sure of the faulty nature of the concept. But it may have sought also (erroneously, given that Napoleonic power was restricted to terra firma, without navy or colonies) to hurt England in her Achilles' heel, which, as the Germans very well understood in the World War, consists not so much in the dependence of the British producer on the continental European consumer, as in the difficulty that England encounters in provisioning her population.[49] With all that, and also admitting the serious political and economic harm that the Continental Blockade caused to many European peoples (as also those of the Italian Kingdom, which Pecchio has referred to in his Storia dell'Amministrazione Finanziaria of that kingdom), who had to put it into practice, it cannot be denied that the Napoleonic measures were beneficial in the long run to a number of industries. And beneficial to France as well, economically speaking, was the work of Napoleon III, the great partisan of Alsatian and Lyonaise industry.

But a better example for reconciling the two terms, autocracy and national wealth, is offered us by the history of our times. It is the example given us by the imperial Germany of William II.

The peoples that afterward were to form the Entente declared war against Germany because of innumerable provocations and oppressions. A madcap emperor and a dominant class, supported by the German people (which, however, could not have given political consent), became megalomaniac and, having fallen in love with the idea of world domination, had for years threatened the world. Once war started, the peoples of the Entente, then all more or less imbued with liberal ideas, went about forming a resistance block "jusqu'au bout" for the following two essential reasons. First, because Germany had shown herself not to be democratic enough. Second, because she had become much too strong and aggressive economically. Far from reciprocally excluding themselves, state autocracy, badly disguised by an impotent and farcical parliamentarism, and economic prosperity attended upon one another in a neat manner in modern Germany.

We shall maintain, consequently, that history teaches us that economic prosperity not only antedates chronologically the existence of democracy, but that it can also happen, after the birth of modern democracy, in states and surroundings ruled by systems other than liberal.

Shall we reverse the thesis, asserting that the preliminary condition of economic prosperity of a nation can be found in its antidemocratic, oligarchic, or absolute system? No, because autocratic governments of the past centuries, as a long and sorrowful experience shows, have too often destroyed, with aggressive wars, what the land had happily gained through the expansion of trade. If the democratic assertion is fallacious, the contrary is not true either. Whether the attainment of economic prosperity can be better achieved by a democratic-liberal regime or by an autocratic one does not seem to me to be precisely and theoretically solvable. It will be necessary in each case to analyze men and things, objects and subjects, times and peoples. "Quod licet Jovi, non licet bovi."

Achille Loria is right, though perhaps exaggerating its importance, when he again and again gives prominence to the importance of historical materialism. Applying this method to the question that here preoccupies us, one cannot fail to see how preponderant economic interests always find a way, whatever may be the external form of the state, to throw their weight on the scale and make their influence felt, employing, in democracy, recurrent demagogic and parliamentarian infiltrations, and in autocratic regimes, interferences and pressure on the government. Yet further research must be made by the student to dissect this intricate and difficult question.

We have already mentioned the existence of an extra-economic psychological, biological, and religious influence on economic matters, which, according to Sombart, favorably predisposes the Hebrew to the acquisition of wealth. And according to studies of Max Weber and Walter Troeltsch, this influence affects also the Protestant mentality—more so the Calvinist (Anglo-Saxon) than the Lutheran (Germanic) —and leads the peoples who follow it to a peak of economic well-being. It would also be helpful to ask what is, for example, the religious and confessional mentality, rather than ask what form of government favors commerce most. At the same time it would not be illicit for the student of social science and economics to raise the great question whether economic welfare is, in every case, the greatest good of a nation, to which any other value should be subordinated. I, for my part, would refuse to subscribe to such an inhuman thesis.

The Interrelation of Economic, Political, and Ideological Causes. Some economic historians, even English ones, strange to say, have given an evaluation of political and ideological forces that sometimes contrasts decisively with the force of economics. They have gone so far as to consider economic history generally as an appendix to political history and, inverting the thesis of Marx, to declare themselves followers of a historical concept, according to which the one would not appear except as a consequence of the latter. To believe W. Cunningham, for example, the whole history of the commerce and industry of Great Britain would be derived from the well-known vicissitudes of political history, as the acts of Edward III, the cruelty of the Duke of Alba against the Dutch, the character of the Stuarts, and so forth. He declares literally that the policy of England never has been a direct effect of economics, but rather it could very well be asserted that the economic life of England has been directly and uninterruptedly influenced by political events. So it is that the configuration of industrial institutions could not substantially be understood save as effects of politics.[50]

According to other English writers it is not capitalism, indeed, that generates bellicose phenomena, but rather bellicosity that generates capitalism. This is, for example, be it only blandly expressed, the thesis of one of the strongest disciples of the Smithian school, MacCulloch, according to whom, without the wars in which England was engaged after the Revolution of 1688, the major part of the resources employed in the struggle never would have been created. According to MacCulloch, the increase in taxes made necessary by war has the same powerful influence on a nation as an increase in his family and its inherent expenses has on an individual. Under the pressure of the war begun in 1799 England intensified her industrial effort and gave proof of a greater spirit of initiative and invention. All the social classes did their best to escape their painful economic condition and production increased. Without doubt, if the taxes had been absolutely oppressive, they would not have had this effect, but they were not heavy enough to produce downheartedness and desperation, although they were heavy enough to make necessary a considerable increase of industry and savings. Without the war against America and the war against France,

concludes MacCulloch, there would have been minor industry and minor frugality, because the need for both would
have been minor. Is it not true perhaps that difficulties sharpen
the intellect?[51]

But MacCulloch perhaps had not read well his teacher
Adam Smith, who said that, if it is true that in the midst of
war's fury the major part of industries can become most prosperous, with the return of peace they can also decline. "They
may flourish amidst the ruin of their country, and begin to
decay upon the return of its prosperity."[52] MacCulloch's thesis
has been reiterated with much new material by a contemporary
German economist, Werner Sombart, in a pertinent book,
War and Capitalism.[53] This was soon followed by a second
one, in which the author endeavored to give prominence to
another profound cause of capitalism and of human efforts:
the woman[54] who, because of her mania for luxury, for the
conquest of man, and the esthetic and social rivalry within
the confines of her own sex has served as a powerful stimulus
for the creation, always more abundant and more refined, of
the means of satisfying her longings.

We certainly will not say that such concepts are completely
devoid of historical truth. We will say only that they incline
to one-sidedness as much as the individualistic version that
considers the story of humanity to be determined solely by the
supposedly imperious (or, as Labriola says, "logical") actions
of fundamental economic laws.[55] In reality, none of the factors that determine historical developments has an exclusive
influence. The complete view of things results from the action
of several forces of dissimilar nature. Nor can even the psycho-
pathic coefficient be excluded from these forces. The contemporary eminent American educator, Charles Merriam, a
profound student of political science, says that it is amazing
indeed that it has not occurred to anyone to write a disserta-
tion about the important function of humor in politics, while,
surely, it would be worth the effort to write a history of the
irrationality *in rebus politicus*, of political folly that is, as the

only suitable means for counterbalancing scientifically the profound treatises on theoretical politics.[56] Does not Charles-Brun tell us that Alexander Dumas' son once refused to write a comedy on some political subject, saying that "Comedy about comedy doesn't go"?[57]

To the followers of the merely diplomatic and archival conception of history we will say then that not even the so-called Cabinet Wars of 1600 and of 1700, wars of invasion, conquest, and caprice, were fundamentally devoid of economic motives. Nor can be omitted the famous aggressive war of Louis XIV of France against Holland in 1672, a war that has been for a long time cited as a typical example of a historical event to be explained only by the "Tel est mon bon plaisir" of a monarch arrogant beyond imagination. In fact, for a while we were satisfied to search for explanations in the pretended irritation of the Bourbon at having been ridiculed by the "gazetteers" of the United Provinces in their newspapers.[58] But now we know that this war occurred as a result not only of the desire to annex the Spanish Netherlands to the dominions of the French monarchy, but from the opinion, prevalent in the industrial classes of the kingdom of France, that it was necessary to bring to a victorious end, with the destruction of Dutch commerce, the tariff struggle that was raging between Holland and her western competitor.

That high government circles knew of this state of mind appears from the following anecdote, related to us by Gourville. A minister of Louis XIV, the Secretary of State, Marquis de Lionne, asked in 1670 of one of his trusted men: "What do you think that one might do to get rid of Dutch commerce?" He promptly replied, "There is nothing else to do but to take Holland itself." The Prince of Condé, present at this dialogue, did not hesitate to declare that he held the same opinion.[59]

Such connections were not hidden to the English economist, who, permeated with a spirit of observation, recognized with Smith that the war of 1672 was caused by the Colbertian protectionist tariff of 1667 and the retaliation measures taken by the Dutch, who assessed high duties on the importation of wines and goods from France.[60] Most economists and historians who adhere to historical materialism have added the limpid water of their good critical sense to the wine of the *Communist Manifesto*. Thus Ettore Ciccotti, in his admirable book on the *Sunset of Slavery* (*Tramonto Della Schiavitu*), has tried carefully to give prominence to the extra-ideological causes of events treated, and has not denied to the other causal elements their efficacy. But to the impenitent disciples of historical materialism we will say finally that the genesis of states, whether they be created by diplomatic assemblies or be spontaneously formed, never is reduced solely to an economic need; and that rather often the genesis of states is in absolute contrast to economic motivation.

Permit us to adduce two examples for the second hypothesis. Economic aspirations (both conscious and unconscious) certainly contributed some part to the movements that brought unity to Germany and Italy. The desire to obtain a greater customs sphere that is needed to develop a great commerce and a powerful industry and the need to smash all the barriers interposed by the small states to the full expansion of competition may be especially mentioned.[61] But on the other side, surely there is no serious historian, regardless of his party affiliations, who would contest that the "magna pars" was due to patriotic sentiment, resting on a linguistic foundation, and to the activity (bound but only very vaguely to the categorical imperative of economics) of the idea of nationality.

In the separation of Belgium from Holland in 1830, economic motivation was particularly evident, because aside from the customs policy of the unified state, the interests of commercial Holland did not tally with those of industrial Belgium, and the tributary fiscal system pressed more heavily upon Belgium than upon Holland.[62] However, the economic reason alone, perhaps, would not have been sufficient for the secession had not various other circumstances been added to it. Above all, it helps to remember the intense religious struggle by reason of which the Flemings, though speaking an idiom more analogous to the Dutch, desired to break away from Calvinist Holland and to make common cause with their Catholic brothers, the French-speaking Walloons. In the second place, the French middle class and their sympathizers in the Belgian provinces, thanks to linguistic and personal contacts with neighboring France, had embraced to a great extent the liberal principles of the French Revolution and of the Napoleonic era, while Holland, isolated, separated from both France and England, was still broadly dominated by conservatives. So that between the two peoples there existed, besides economic antagonism, two other powerful incongruities of a mental and religious nature which were not of economic origin.

In consideration of the first hypothesis enunciated, that is, that the genesis of some states may be rather simply the result of diplomatic assemblies, we will observe that perhaps even this may be capable of some proof.

Among the most elementary conclusions of historical research is the fact that, especially from the fourteenth century to the beginning of the nineteenth, the formation of states occurred on the basis of dynastic arrangements independently of the economic conditions of the countries involved. Austria, the offspring of adroit matrimonial politics—"et tu, felix Austria, nube"—considered from the economic point of view, never had a reason to come to exist. Spain, composed of Catalonia and Castile, welded together by a royal marriage, constitutes a truly geographic expression. So little of the economic is there in the union that the separatist faction among the Catalonians has since the seventeenth century aimed at a clear division of its land from the western regions, believed by it to be deeply foreign, not only on the linguistic and cultural side, but also because of their greatly retarded economic-social development.

In modern wars, during which economic motives operate visibly, there yet act contemporaneously a series of other factors. Modern wars, for example, are produced almost always by the aroused moral sentiments of the modern masses, although impulses of an economic nature are present. This happened even in the typical capitalistic war of the English to conquer the diamond fields of the Transvaal. A second cause existed, at least equal in importance to the economic, in the age-old hatred of the Dutch, long established in the land, for the English parvenus, and in the struggle for South African supremacy between the two peoples, otherwise racially and religiously related.

Remaining on economic ground, little or nothing divided France and Germany before the World War. There had been, to be sure, the German attempt, we will say, to share the benefits derived from the conquest of Morocco, that France, with much alacrity and energy, had been enjoying since 1904. The attempt, made ineptly and inadequately, left in the two peoples a long trail of misunderstandings and bitterness and, therefore, served to rekindle slumbering antagonism. Yet, more than creating or even only revealing an economic antagonism, the attempt only recalled the harm that the two nations had done each other in the political history of centuries gone by, and above all presented again the painful question of Alsace-Lorraine. Achille Loria views the economic reason for the war between Germany and France as a struggle for possession of the metalliferous fields, the deposits of iron and the layers of coal, located pickaback between the two states, in the region between the Meuse and the Rhine. He points out that in the rest of Europe iron and coal are far apart.

We will confess that those are not our views. As the same Loria safely urges, limiting the importance of the antagonism revealed by him, we must be careful not to fall into the stale and discredited prejudice that a nation cannot develop a given industry unless she has political sovereign authority over all or most of the regions that produce its raw materials.[63] Rather, Calwer was right when, in the presence of a great number of French and German economists, he stated that, be it as producers of articles of exportation, the form and substance of which were nearly always dissimilar, or be it for their common economic, maritime, and colonial antagonism against England, the two states, Germany and France, far from being divided by conflicting economic interests, complemented each other in a most happy manner. The collision between Germany and France, without which the World War hardly would have broken out and, even if it had, would not have become global, is a phenomenon eminently historical, in the psychological and political sense of the word.

Consequently, we could sum up the method to follow in historico-political and historico-economic research in the precept that the student should extract, in each case, all the obsolete and current ideological motives and look for the economic roots of the phenomenon to analyze. But at the same time the student must remain well aware of the fact encountered in phenomenology, be it individual or collective, that there also exist unlimited coefficients of a dissimilar nature. The difficulty of the task incumbent upon the philosopher of history lies in examining the single case, whose research he undertakes etiologically. That is, he must disentangle the determining causes; he must establish their multiple character and the relations existing among them; he must define, limit, and verify the different measures of participation by certain qualitative elements known a priori, such as the economic factor, race, tradition, and others. Put another way, he must eviscerate the problem with the object of tracing, with care and precision, the quantitative proportions of qualitatively pre-established coefficients.

NOTES

1. Alberto de' Stefani, *La Dinamica Patrimoniale nell' odierna economia capitalistica*, Padova: "La Litotipo," 1921, p. 128.
2. Georg Simmel, *Ueber soziale Differenzierung: Soziologische und psychologische Untersuchungen*, Leipzig: Duncker, 1890, pp. 100–106.

3. Roberto Michels, *La Sociologia del Partito Politico nella Democrazia Moderna. Studi sulle tendenze oligarchiche degli aggregati politici,* Turin: Utet, 1912, p. 366. Also see my *Storia critica del movimento socialista italiano, dagli inizi fino al 1911,* Florence: Voce, 1926, p. 53.

4. M. Pantaleoni, *Erotemi di Economia,* Bari: Laterza, 1924.

5. Tocqueville, *De la Démocratie en Amérique, loc. cit.,* Vol. I, Part II, pp. 216–218.

6. Gerhard von Schulze-Gaevernitz, *Freie Meere,* Stuttgart-Berlin: Deutsche Verlagsanstalt, 1915, p. 11; Gustavus Myers, *History of the Great American Fortunes* (German ed., Berlin: Fischer, 1916, Vol. I, p. 266) describes Vanderbilt as one of the types analyzed in the text.

7. Tocqueville, *loc. cit.,* Vol. I, Part II, p. 250.

8. Kurt Wiedenfeld, *Das Persönliche im modernen Unternehmertum,* Leipzig: Duncker, 1911, p. 11.

9. Edmond About, *Le progrès,* Paris: Hachette, 1864, p. 56. Cf. also, Charles Gide in his essay: "De la nécessité pour la France d'accroître sa production," *Revue d'économie politique,* 1916, p. 336.

10. Corrado Gini, "Problemi di Economia politica visti da uno statistico," *Annali di Economia,* Milan: Università Bocconi, Vol. I, 1924–1925, p. 259.

11. Vilfredo Pareto, *Manuel d'économie politique,* Paris: Giard, 1909, p. 18.

12. *Ibid.,* p. 29.

13. Maffeo Pantaleoni, *Scritti vari di economia,* third series, Rome: Castellani, 1910, p. 63.

14. Giovanni Lorenzoni, *Inchiesta sulle condizioni del lavoro,* Milan: Ufficio del Lavoro, 1904, Vol. I, p. 34. He points out that during the rice-husking season, the wives of the sharecroppers also come down from the hills.

15. Francesco Pullè, *Resoconto,* Congresso Nazionale dei Lavoratori della Terra, Bologna, 1901, Bologna: Azzoguidi, 1902, p. 22.

16. In the Twentieth Century, the Manchester Channel Company had 40,000 share holders, and Lipton had 74,262 (Eduard Bernstein, *Die Voraussetzungen des Sozialismus,* p. 48). Cf. also Robert Liefmann, *Geschichte und Kritik des Sozialismus,* Leipzig: Quelle, 1922, p. 135.

17. Heinrich Herkner, *Die Arbeiterfrage,* 5th ed., Berlin: Guttentag, 1908, p. 497.

18. Max Weber in the first German Sociological Convention at Frankfort, October 1910. Cf. *Frankfurter Zeitung,* No. 292, p. 2.

19. Max Weber, *Gesammelte Aufsätze zur Religionssoziologie,* Vol. I, Tübingen: Mohr, 1920, p. 17ff.

20. W. Sombart, *Der moderne Kapitalismus,* Leipzig, 1902, Vol. II, p. 349, Vol. I, pp. 266ff, also Sombart, *Der Bourgeois,* Munich: Buncker, 1913.

21. Voltaire, *Siècle de Louis XIV,* Paris: Diderot, 1864, p. 419.

22. Ettore Rota, "Quel che la Germania deve alla Francia," *Rivista delle Nazioni Latine,* Vol. III, No. 15, Dec. 1, 1918, p. 323.

23. *Mémoires de Monsieur D'Ablancourt, envoyè de Sa Majesté Très-Chrétienne Louis XIV en Portugal, contenant l'histoire de Portugal depuis le Traité des Pyrénées de 1657 jusqu'à 1668,* The Hague: Ellinckhuysen, 1701, p. 18.

24. Pecchio, *Saggio storico sulla amministrazione finanziera,* pp. 118–119.

25. Alexander von Peez und Paul Dehn, *Englands Vorherrschaft: Aus der Zeit der Kontinentalsperre*, Leipzig: Duncker, 1912, pp. 270–284; Bein, *Die Industrie des Sächsischen Vogtlandes*, Leipzig: Koenig, 1884; *Die sächsische Baumwollindustrie am Ende des vorigen Jahrhunderts und während der Kontinentalsperre*, Leipzig, 1889; Zimmerman, *Blüte und Verfall des Leinengewerbes in Schlesien*, Breslau, 1888.
26. Mathieu Schwann, *Geschichte der Kölner Handelskammer*, Cologne: Neubner, 1906, p. 289.
27. *Ibid.*, p. 289.
28. *Ibid.*, p. 315.
29. *Ibid.*, p. 401.
30. *Ibid.*, p. 393.
31. Henry Laufenburger, *L'industrie sidérurgique de la Lorraine désannexée et la France*, Strasbourg: Berger-Levrault, 1924, p. 251.
32. Otto Beck, *Die Wirtschafts-Gebiete an der Mittel-Donau vor dem Kriege*, Vienna: Verlag für Fachliteratur, 1922, pp. 8, 10–11, 117, 119.
33. Paolo Paruta, *Opere Politiche*, Florence: Le Monnier, 1852, Vol. II, pp. 218ff.
34. M. Huet, *Histoire du Commerce et de la Navigation*, 2nd ed., Paris: Constelier, 1716, p. 272.
35. *Ibid.*, pp. 120–121.
36. Francesco Mengotti, *Del Commercio dei Romani dalla prima guerra punica a Costantino*, Padova: Seminario, 1787, p. 3.
37. Guillaume-Thomas Raynal, *Histoire Philosophique et Politique des Etablissements et du Commerce Européens dans les deux Indes*, The Hague: Gosse, 1776, Chap. CXXI.
38. Mengotti, pp. 19, 137; also G. Pecchio, *Storia dell'Economia pubblica in Italia ossia Epilogo critico degli Economisti italiani*, 3rd ed., Lugano: Tip. della Svizzera italiana, 1849, pp. 212–213.
39. Adolfo Asturaro, *Il materalismo storico e la sociologia generale*, Genoa: Libreria moderna, 1904, p. 293.
40. These relationships have been thoroughly developed in my book: *La Sociologia del Partito Politico*, pp. 248ff.
41. Edouard Berth, *Les méfaits des intellectuels*, Paris: Rivière, 1914, p. 223.
42. Gaetano Mosca, *Elementi di Scienza politica*, 2nd ed., Turin: Bocca, 1923; and *Teorica dei Governi e Governo parlamentare*, 2nd ed., Milan, Istituto Editoriale Scientifico. (EDITOR'S NOTE: The American translation of Mosca's work is called *The Ruling Class*, New York: McGraw-Hill, 1939.)
43. Gaetano Mosca, "La crisi della democrazia esaminata da Roberto Michels," *Corriere della Sera*, Anno L., No. 205 (August 29, 1915).
44. Achille Loria, "Democrazia e Duci," *Echi e Commenti*, Anno VI, No. 21 (July 25, 1925).
45. Antonio Genovesi, *Lezioni di Commercio ossia de Economia Civile*, Milan: Silvestri, 1820, p. 356.
46. Smith, *op. cit.*, p. 427.
47. Antonio Zanon, *Lettere scelte sull'Agricoltura, sul Commercio e sulle Arti*, Milan: Destefanis, 1804.
48. Smith, *op. cit.*, p. 532.
49. Hermann Levy, *Die neue Kontinentalsperre. Ist Grossbritannien wirtschaftlich bedroht?* Berlin: Springer, 1915.

50. W. Cunningham, *The Growth of English Industry and Commerce in Modern Times*, Cambridge: 1905, p. 9.
51. MacCulloch, *The Principles of Political Economy, with some Inquiries respecting their Application*, 5th ed., Edinburgh: Black, 1864.
52. Smith, p. 409.
53. Werner Sombart, *Krieg und Kapitalismus*, Munich: Duncker und Humblot, 1913.
54. Werner Sombart, *Luxus und Kapitalismus*, Munich: Duncker und Humblot, 1913.
55. Arturo Labriola, *Il capitalismo*, Turin: Bocca, 1910.
56. Charles E. Merriam, "Progress in Political Research," *American Political Science Review*, Vol. XX, 1(1926), p. 5.
57. *Le roman social en France au XIX siècle*, Paris: Giard et Brière, 1910, p. 229.
58. "Il pousse le mépris des hommes jusqu'à faire la guerre pour une médaille," thus typically expresses himself in his rather lucid treatise Pierre-Edouard Lémontey, *Essai sur l'établissement monarchique de Louis XIV*, Paris: Déterville, 1818, p. 376.
59. *Mémoires de Monsieur de Gourville concernant les affaires actuelles auxquelles il a été employé par la cour depuis 1642 jusqu'en 1698*, Paris, 1724, Vol. II, p. 159.
60. Smith, *op. cit.*, p. 430.
61. Read for Italy the interesting sketches by Arnaldo Agnelli, "Il Materialismo storico e il Risorgimento italiano," *Rendiconto del Reale Istituto Lombardo di Scienze e Lettere*, Vol. XLVI, fasc. 5 (1913), and Giuseppe Prezzolini, "Fattori economici nel Risorgimento italiano," *Voce*, Anno III, No. 1 (1911).
62. Camille Huysmans, Louis de Brouckère et Louis Bertrand, *75 Années de Domination bourgeoise, 1830–1905*, Ghent: Volksdrukkereij, 1905.
63. Achille Loria, *Aspetti sociali ed economici della guerra mondiale*, Milan: Vallardi, 1921, p. 17.

CHAPTER III

The Elite

THE doctrine of the "circulation of the elites" enunciated by Vilfredo Pareto can be considered one of the most remarkable theories of the philosophy of history of recent times. This theory, briefly, maintains that no association can do without a dominant class, but that the dominant classes undergo rapid decay. At first they become enervated; then they experience a process of dissolution; finally they morally and physically succumb and yield the field to a new dominant class that arises from the people.

The people as a collectivity never can democratically govern itself, but the rulers themselves change continually.[1] However it seems possible for us to assert, on the basis of several recent historical researches on the subject, that the process analyzed by Pareto perhaps happens less in the form of *absolute exchange*, than in that of a *perennial amalgamation* of new elements with the old ones.

It may be helpful to penetrate the core of the Paretian theory. It is founded above all on the intrinsic impossibility of popular rule. To such a question we have already dedicated our book on *Political Parties*, to which we should like to refer the reader. Furthermore it is based on the premise of the weak biological vitality or the social, moral, and economic decadence of the aristocracy. It is appropriate therefore to ask ourselves to what extent this last thesis corresponds to the facts known to us.

For many centuries the nobility, titled or minor, was a

dominating element of the aristocracy. The sociological problem of the elite as a ruling class may be put therefore in these
terms: Does the old nobility exist still? And, in the affirmative,
does it still hold socially, economically, and bio-genealogically
the same position it held centuries ago?

We shall examine first the question of aristocratic vitality.
All research up to now on this point has occurred in restricted
fields and, therefore, does not yet, in any way, permit a generalization of the results.

We will bring up some examples. In Sweden, King Gustavus Adolphus in 1626 founded a so-called House of Nobility,
to which any nobleman who wanted to be counted and recognized as such had to belong. Each noble family received a
genealogical table, on which all the events concerning it and
all the changes in the social state of its members such as births,
marriages, deaths, etc., were registered. In this way the House
of Nobility functioned for the Swedish aristocracy as a sort
of census and statistical office, so that it is now in a position
to offer to demographers a quantity of most precious
knowledge. The credit for having taken up and made use of
this important resource belongs to Fahlbeck (1900).[2]

From 1626 to 1898 there have existed in Sweden alto-
gether 3033 families belonging to the nobility (142 in commendam, 417 baronial, 2474 noble without any title); of
these, 2319 became extinct in the lapse of time indicated,
that is, 82 in commendam, 277 baronial, and 1965 simple
nobles. In other words, and this is for us the most conspicuous
point of Fahlbeck's researches, in about two hundred seventy
years 76.6 per cent disappeared, that is to say, more than two-
thirds.

Another interesting point from Fahlbeck's research is that
of the 2319 families that disappeared in the indicated period
of time, only 137 can be traced back to the epoch prior to
1626, while all the others were ennobled later. This fact would
give value to the thesis that ancient noble families are endowed with a greater vitality than the new ones. The Swedish

researches, in fact, seem to show that the mortality of the families, instead of growing with their age, diminishes. The younger families (and the adjective "younger" here is intended always in the social sense and not in the biological sense of the word) are much more exposed to decay. For the aristocracy, youth can be said to be the most critical age. Of each one thousand noble families that disappeared, 439 became extinct in the first 25 years of their existence as a noble family, and only 206 after a duration of 126–150 years.[8]

From these figures, however, it will not be permissible to draw conclusions without some caution. It is known from experience that the bestowal of diplomas of nobility usually happens with more facility when the "pater familias" being ennobled has no children or, at least, has no excessive number of them. This is first of all so as not to infuse into the aristocracy too much new blood at one time. It is done also because in families rich in offspring, more often than in those with few progeny, it happens that there is some son, whose moral or even political behavior is not such as to counsel the prince to accept the father—and with him the scamp son—into the ranks of the nobility. That explains to a certain extent the reason why the percentage of those families newly ennobled who disappear shortly thereafter is so high.

Yet this circumstance by itself is not sufficient to clarify the total picture of decline. There will be, naturally, the hypothesis of moral degeneration, with its physiological consequences. Fahlbeck would exclude *a priori* this explanation. According to him the Swedish nobility as a class has been neither decadent nor impoverished. On the contrary, to Fahlbeck, with justification, physiological degeneration alone seems to be the reason.[4] This last is particularly reflected in the high percentage of sterile marriages, in the small number of children that are born from those fertile, and in the great mortality of the male progeny. Moreover, among the causes of the extinction of the Swedish noble families is enumerated the fact that celibacy was very common. Of each 100 male children born to the disappearing nobility, hardly 30 married.[5]

The following table reveals the percentage of sterile marriages in the Swedish nobility:

Noble Families Lasting	Percentage of Sterile Marriages in the					
	1st Gen.	2nd Gen.	3rd Gen.	4th Gen.	5th Gen.	6th Gen.
2 generations	13.72	63.68				
3 generations	8.76	19.64	64.15			
4 generations	10.75	17.09	20.79	62.07		
5 generations	18.31	17.09	23.08	21.36	75.00	
6 generations	10.26	10.00	19.35	14.29	17.07	70.00

As this table shows, of each 100 marriages of male progeny of the generation in course of extinction, from about 62 to 75 have had no descent. How much the low fecundity has contributed to the disappearance of the family is shown by the fact that in the last generation of the vanishing families the average of children born from each fruitful marriage was only 1.00 to 2.67. The mortality of the male progeny under 19 years of age in the last generation was between 40 and 50 per cent.

We will briefly point to some other examples. Even before the middle of the nineteenth century, the Marquis Benoiston de Châteauneuf attempted to prove that in France the average age of the noble families did not exceed three centuries. The causes which he adduces to explain this phenomenon are the right of primogeniture and the consequent tendency toward impoverishment of the cadets, the marriages between blood relations with their ensuing sterility, the duelling mania with which the nobility was afflicted, and above all, war, which decimated the males of the French nobility.[6] The prominence given by some writers to the fact that wars serried to a great extent the ranks of the French nobility is certainly correct.[7]

By far the greatest part of them "would choose no other profession than the military" as the Marquis de Fenquieres, famous scientific writer on military affairs, said in 1717.[8] We will also report the example of the Choiseul family, related to us by Louandre, that during the reign of Louis XIV alone lost a clear twenty-eight of its members on the battlefield.[9] However, to account for the relatively short average duration of some noble families there must have been additional general reasons also. For the same Benoiston de Châteauneuf arrived at analogous conclusions, too, in his research on the longevity of the middle class and of the small proprietors, who in those times did not espouse the profession of arms.[10]

This last indication by Châteauneuf of the brief duration of middle-class families is corroborated also by other research. At Mannheim (in Germany) Schott completed some studies in regard to 1000 families residing in that city in the year 1719. Of these families, he discovered in 1900, after a period of 181 years, only 99 remaining, about one-tenth.[11] In other words, nine-tenths had been lost in the lapse of not even two centuries. Of the 1461 families existing in 1807–1811, in 1900, 89 years later, there were but 563 left, which represents a little more than a third.[12] Since several of the families stemming from 1807 are found in 1900 to be subdivided into a certain number of derived families, or branches, it is possible to calculate that at the beginning of 1900 there existed in all, in round numbers, 1300 old Mannheimian families, relatively "authentic."[13]

Inasmuch as the research of Schott deals with the ancient families exclusively in a chronological sense and not in the social, it is not a very relevant contribution to the question of the antiquity of the aristocratic families and therefore of the continuity of the political class. For the families of day laborers are ancient also, so far as concerns their histories since 1807. It is not even easy to ascertain then how many of the 563 families indicated as surviving were descendants of the old ruling classes. Rather, whoever scrutinizes the lists of names may convince himself that the families taken as a test belong prevailingly to the working class and to the small proprietor class. Among the 543 families dwelling in Mannheim from 1807 to 1900, there is but one of noble rank (the von Fischer).[14]

Supposing that this last datum is exact, we would be tempted to infer that the vitality of Mannheim's nobility is absolutely nil.[15] But the fact should be mentioned that exactly at the beginning of the period taken into consideration, the city of Mannheim was struck by an event that must have exercised not only a profound influence over the social characteristics of the city, but that also must have had some most important consequences in a demographic sense, that is, the moving of the seat of the Grand Duchy government to Karlsruhe. This fact caused a great part of the nobility to abandon the city for the new capital. Consequently, the social composition of the ruling classes in Mannheim was greatly modified.

The major value of studies such as those by Schott lies not so much in the light that they throw on the problem of the duration of families as in the help that they may give us in determining the degree of mobility or, to express ourselves in a positive sense, of local stability or "sedentariness" of the various fractions of the population. Schott really does not furnish us the least explanation in regard to the fate of the ancient families of Mannheim who in 1900 no longer figured in the census. Nor does one come to know how many of them had become extinct and how many instead had only transferred their residence somewhere else. That the number of these last must have been conspicuous is implicitly admitted by Schott himself, when he advises that at Mannheim the major part of the derived families that had disappeared, precisely 73.6 per cent, were no longer verifiable, at least in the male branch, in the second generation.[16] It is then significant that the transfer of the capital from Mannheim to Karlsruhe had been effected exactly midway in the life of the first generation, taken for test purposes by our author as of the year 1801.

It is well to stop on one more point still: the problem of the daughters' descent. For the female descendants who marry lose their name, and consequently are not considered, statistically, as belonging to the family. Even the important Swedish statistics are silent, too, in this regard. And yet this problem is of the greatest importance for the question of the preservation of aristocracy through the persistence of the blood. A flourishing family, belonging to the aristocracy for many centuries, can, even if blessed with ten children, become lineally extinguished whenever among these ten children not a single male child remains. If it has nothing but ten daughters, it becomes extinguished *ipso facto*.[17] Given the case that all ten daughters marry, and that all these marriages are prolific, we have truly as a result that, notwithstanding the statistical disappearance of the family for lack of male offspring, the blood is renovated with most exceptional strength. Here the biological concept of the family is in irrepressible contradiction with the juridico-statistical.

The question imposes itself, then, whether a great part of that category of the old ruling class that the most imperfect statistics give as extinct is not surviving still in its feminine descent, particularly in the actual dominant class. Thus, statistics present some almost insurmountable obstacles. Everyone knows that the continuity of families which form the dominant classes is often assured precisely by girls belonging to the old extractions who, through marriage, enter new families. If the noble families that see themselves threatened in the masculine branch, for some reason or other (and especially for economic motives) do not find a husband for their daughter in the circle of families belonging to their own social rank, they naturally will look for one in the circle of those middle-class families that, having recently become rich and illustrious, will presumably find themselves shortly elevated to the same hierarchic conditions.

However the ancient noble blood is not lost, but is transfused in the veins of the rising aristocracy. There is often continuity of blood even where there is no longer a continuity of name. Sometimes, it is true, the name may be retained. This occurs whenever the last lineal descendants of families of a very illustrious line obtain from the monarch a special grant to enable them to transmit their own name to the husband or to the children. It is well understood that these cases are very rare and hardly detract from the rule of the genealogical feminine "sacrifice."

Putting aside descent of "blood" and dealing again with names, one still cannot believe that the ancient nobility has disappeared from the surface of the earth. Whatever is said about its low vitality, it still exists now and affirms itself in an active manner. In fact there are always found in the world, at the height of society, not a few exponents of famous historical names. Particularly in *rebus politicus*, aristocracy has not yet ceased to exist. That the parties of the right enumerate among their leaders a great number of eminent nobles is a thing that, given the conservative character of aristocracy, should not be astonishing in the least. But it is worthy of note that the parties of the extreme left often have some noble as their leader. We know that in the great French Revolution, which turned with considerable violence against the aristocracy of blood, the great parties of opposition, and even those of the Revolution, were led by exiles of the French nobility: Mirabeau, the Abbé de Sieyès, Lafayette, Condorcet, Robespierre, the "ci-devants" Philippe Egalite, Saint-Just, Collot d'Herbois, Hérault de Séchelles. Also among the leaders of the modern labor "movement" the noble element abounds, especially at its inception. So we have seen in Russia, Bakunin, Lavroff, Kropotkin; in Italy, Pisacane, Cafiero, Covelli. Nor have things changed much in more recent times. In Germany the Socialist fraction of the Bavarian Landtag was for a certain time led by two aristocrats of blood, who were besides the only ones in the entire Landtag, Vollmar and Haller.

Passing to the ambit of middle-class politics in prewar Italy, we see that the government of many of the major cities was in the hands of men descending from hereditary titles. At Venice the mayor was a Grimani, at Florence a Corsini, at Rome a Colonna. In parliament one of the Roman electoral colleges was represented by a Caetani, another by a Borghese. In the parliamentary representation of the Italian Radical Party the middle and high nobility, including some Roman princes, were predominant. In the same period, the control of the British government was held by a Grey, a Balfour, and a Churchill. In the German army, which, as is known, for military valor was not the last in the world, 80 per cent of the army-corps commanders were members of the old feudal nobility. It was calculated that in the cavalry two-thirds of the lieutenants, three-fourths of the captains, four-fifths of the majors, six-sevenths of the colonels and major-generals, seven-eighths of the lieutenant-generals, and all the generals were of noble lineage.[18]

The World War was useful in corroborating in large measure our assertion, for it gave to the old aristocracy occasion to strengthen its ancient abilities.

In France the nobility furnished absolute proof of its valor. At the side of citizen Joffre were some noble leaders of first rank. There were de Castelnau, de Grandmaison, de Villaret, Langh de Cary, de Mand'hui, d'Urbal, de Franchet d'Esperey, Hely d'Oissel, de Mas-Latrie, Boué de Lapeyrére and others. Given the extreme caution that the French republican government, for obvious political motives, shows in resorting to the nobles for filling high positions in the army, the frequency of so many gentlemen among the military chiefs is clothed for them with a doubly significant and flattering character.[19]

In England, too, aristocracy, well known to be not so numerous, paid a very large tribute to war. As can be seen in the lists of the fallen in December 1915, 800 noblemen died on the battlefield, among them a member of the royal family, the prince of Battenberg, 6 peers, 16 baronets, 6 knights, and 7 members of parliament, 164 companions of the order of cavalry, 95 sons of peers, 82 sons of baronets, and 34 sons of knights. At the end of 1916 some of these figures were greatly increased: 18 peers, 21 baronets, 200 knights, 118 heirs of grand titles of nobility.[20] One cannot say then that in England the rich were sending the poor to die in the war, for the percentage of the fallen aristocrats was higher than that of the other social classes.

In Germany, Hindenburg was a Junker. In Italy, the high military command was entrusted to the hand of a Cadorna, and the conquest of Gorizia was due, besides to him, to General Count Marazzi. The sacrifice, after the battle of Caporetto, of two regiments of cavalry, whose officers were mostly young men belonging to the high aristocracy, was such as to fill the survivors with just pride. The words attributed to the officers in the act of counterattacking the advancing enemy may be remembered: "If the plebians run away, it is up to the gentlemen to show them how to die and restore the honor of the country."[21]

In its origin, the nobility is clothed with a class character that demands not only power but also wealth. Sombart affirms for Germany that to the nobility itself a certain degree of wealth seems a natural attribute, psychologically and socially congenital with nobility. However, the kind and use of wealth are more important than its quantity.[22] But, among the German petty nobility, less provided with means, wealth is not at all taken for granted and permeates their thinking. In certain parts of Sicily the terms noble and rich are synonymous.[23] The people instinctively presuppose wealth in the nobility, and when that is lacking hold the nobles in contempt. In Tuscany the proverb runs: "A count without a county is like a flask without wine."[24] It is a fact, furthermore, that conspicuous fractions of the nobility in Italy, in Germany, in Spain, and elsewhere, live in very modest conditions and sometimes very close to poverty. The same conditions prevail in the France of Poitou where "the race of good families does not disappear; it falls into decay."[25] As D'Avenel said of France in general, many families that for some time were rising "have plunged back into the crowd, and many families believed to have been extinguished, merely have disappeared."[26] In the Latin countries especially, it often happens that impoverished noble families, because of pride or because their noble title becomes an insupportable burden, or even for reasons of a political nature, give up bearing a title. Therefore there occurs in these cases economic decadence, not biological extinction.

And we will say further that the causes of economic decadence of a part of the nobility are various. The traditional pride and the contempt of things mercantile as being contrary to the dignity of truly good families have led many noble families to ruin. Others have been ruined by an elegant and lavish life beyond the limits of their means. Still others have decided to give themselves up to industry, but have done poorly because of their lack of skill and because of fickleness. And many others have become impoverished in the service of the state.[27]

Undoubtedly the average nobility, even if it has retained possession of its real property or at least of its patrimony, has been nowadays driven back into a secondary role by the upper ranks of the productive middle class wherever modern industry has been established. But it is also true that this finding is not valid in all situations. The base of the financial power of the nobility is not, indeed, so much in capital as in its possession of land and mansions. We will speak first of the palaces in the city. The patrician palaces not rarely pass from hands of ancient families to other hands. Even here the sons often have not known how to preserve either the splendor of the name nor the father's property. They have been reduced to the painful necessity of selling (for a good price) the inherited palace to purchase a more modest dwelling.

Impoverishment was not the only cause of this phenomenon. To understand this, it suffices to bear in mind how modern cities developed. The old nobility was tempted to give up the occupancy of its palaces which were located mostly in the center of the city. Not the least among the causes that enticed the nobles to abandon their ancient, beautiful, but unhealthy, outdated, and uncomfortable city houses was modern private hygiene, which seemed to invite the tenants of houses located in dark and narrow lanes to emigrate to the verdant suburbs, where there was more light and more air. Nor should one neglect the mania of profit which afflicted many proprietors, even those who owned palaces, when they perceived that the price of land was continually increasing. So to make money, though without any need of it, they sold the centuries-old cradles of their family.[28] In many cases such action may very well be thought to be in bad taste and contrary to the respect and the "pietas" dear to the Romans, that pious devotion owing to the forefathers and their concrete and often glorious works. It may also be ventured that the new residences are almost always far inferior to the ancient palaces with their patriarchal nobility and elegant appearance, apart from that synthesis of grandiosity and sobriety which imposes social respect and artistic admiration. Thus a change of habitation is by no means always a sign of poverty.

But the real strength of aristocracy consists in its agrarian roots. Especially where a part of the landed property happens to be in the hands of noble families in an inalienable form, as so-called "bonded property" (gebundener Grundbesitz), the dissolution of the aristocracy encounters a powerful barrier. The fidei commissa, forbidding the sale of land to third parties, have been abolished in France and in Italy. They are to be considered as an eminently feudal institution. That is, they are part of a political regime and of an economic system both precapitalistic. They obviously interpose serious stumbling blocks to the development of a wholesome agrarian economy, be it in a private sense or in a social sense. The persistence of the fidei commissum of prewar times was undoubtedly a symptom of the "dualism" which characterized German political life, but it constituted also an unshakable foundation for the economic welfare of a conspicuous part of the aristocracy and contributed much to the continuity and the stability of the Junkers.[29]

But, if wealth often is a phenomenon that accompanies aristocratic power, it today does not form its political base at all. It is furthermore needless to say that the power of the aristocracy does not spring from democracy and from parliamentarism. In Germany, for example, the nobleman did not need to hold the reins of political power or control the parliamentarian majority. In case of necessity, the influence exercised by his social position sufficed, along with the family's traditions, his military attributes, and also his intrigues. The so-called German revolution weakened the authority of the noble class. But much less than is commonly believed. A curious phenomenon, first pointed out by Wittich, is that the World War was instrumental in rendering the conditions of a considerable part of the German aristocracy, especially those of the landed interest, more prosperous than before. The German Republic had to reckon with some Junkers even more powerful than those of the monarchy that preceded it.[30]

THE ABSORPTION OF NEW ELEMENTS BY THE HEREDITARY ARISTOCRACY

The theory of the alternation of the superior classes, the "circulation of the elites," is then susceptible of two complementary additions or at least of two points of greater development. First, we have observed that the old aristocracy does not disappear, does not founder, does not become proletarian or impoverished (at least not in an absolute sense), does not "make way" for new groups of rulers, but that it always remains at the head of nations which it led over the course of centuries.

In the second place, the old aristocracy, be it very old or rejuvenated, does not exercise the rule alone but is forced to share it with some kind of new ruler. These would be the recent nobility of government employees, ennobled for services rendered to the state, the leaders of the more or less recently titled plutocracy, the baptized Hebrew merchants and bankers and those non-baptized, and sometimes even some scientists. All these are in some degree, yes, polished, but partly they are also morally and physically "hirsute and uncombed" still. To say it in a few words, nowadays the aristocracy of birth, already by and for itself profoundly altered, is accompanied by an aristocracy of government clerks, an aristocracy of money, and an aristocracy of knowledge. Put together, these constitute aristocracy in the sense of a ruling class. New elements continually infiltrate into the formerly feudal aristocracy, and make imposing claims to a place in the sun at its side.

It is certain that such emulation by the inferior classes requires of them a not inconsiderable expenditure of energy; and, in their attempts to raise themselves, not only can they not help appearing awkward, but sometimes, lacking sufficient power, they may miserably fail and directly succumb.

Criticism, then, has never been wanting on the part of scientists, nor witticism and irony on the part of poets and playwrights. To cite only a few examples, we will mention a French observer of the period of Louis XIV, a pupil of Colbert, Jacques Savary, who warned that members of the middle class of his time often ruined themselves, so given were they to exorbitant expenditure and great shows in imitation of the nobles.[31] The ridiculous side of this ambition may be seen in the immortal humorous comedy by Moliere, "Le Bourgeois Gentilhomme," and there comes to mind La Fontaine's fable, the moral of the frog which wanted to become as big as the ox:

> "The world is full of men no more sage:
> Each bourgeois emulates the grand seigneurs
> Each petty prince has his ambassadors
> Each marquis wants to have his page!"

However, such an interpretation of the social tendency of upward mobility may be dubious. Recently the type of the

French "bourgeois gentilhomme" has found, very unexpect-
edly, a panegyrist in the person of a sociologist, René Johannet, according to whom M. Jourdain constitutes a type
clothed in such serious attributes as good sense, brightness of
ideas, simplicity, courage, and sincerity. If Jourdain declares
that he does not intend to stay "always at the bottom" and
that he longs to pass to a social class superior to his own,
Johannet insists that this shows that Jourdain is not only a
civilized person, but a propagator of civility.[32] Nor did our
author hesitate to praise the French nobility of the "*ancien
regime*" who, by not refusing to welcome "le bourgeois gentilhomme" to its ranks, had given proof of being gifted with
great sagacity. It allowed a revolution to be made "from the
top" to prevent its being made "from the bottom."[33]

However it may be that in the pure aristocratic orders the
political class is, so to speak, a closed hereditary class, difficult
of entry, exclusive and stable, it would be erroneous to think
that, in the manner of an Indian caste, the political class is
impenetrable. Rather, it is not able to maintain itself except
by giving up its purity. Aristocracy, through a steady infiltra-
tion of new forces, has been subjected at all times to a process
of biological and social renewal. Nobility has always been rejuvenated by the entry of heterogeneous elements of the
middle class. To illustrate the thesis expounded, we will give
several examples.

When, in the second half of the century of Louis XIV a
vigorous French middle class arose, it did not know how better
to adapt itself to the old environment than to take as a model
the customs and the way of life, the manners, and the very
mentality of the feudal class. It thereby succeeded to a great
extent in being received to the bosom of the aristocracy. The
eminent bourgeoisie, having been admitted to the service of
the state, whose high offices were yet prevalently invested with
the character of noble privilege, would soon change their
given name and family name. The Fouquet, the Le Tellier,
the Colbert, the Philippeaux, the Desmarets, become the

Belle-Isle, the de Louvois, the de Seignelay, the de Maurepas, the de Lavrillere, and the de Maillebois.[34]

Not only the recently-formed middle class but even the "noblesse de robe" exercised its ambitions for social climbing by keeping itself in most intimate contact with the "noblesse d'epee." This is evident in the most valuable memoir of the Abbé de Choisy, who received from his mother the precious advice not to frequent any but the drawing rooms of the "noblesse d'epee," even though, his forefathers having held the high offices of Maitre des Requetes and of Conseiller d'Etat, he himself belonged to the "noblesse de robe."[35]

In modern Germany for over a half century we have witnessed the process of absorption of the young industrial middle class by the old hereditary aristocracy, a process that is being accomplished with enormous celerity.[36] The German middle class is feudalizing itself to the point that it exists almost as a socially independent middle class, proud of itself, in the sense of possessing that which the French call "l'esprit de corps." But the relative emancipation of the commoners has only resulted in strengthening its original enemy, the nobility, infusing it with new blood and new economic forces.

The enriched middle class aspires to nothing else than intimate association with the nobles. This they certainly may accomplish through marriage with aristocratic girls, for thereby they avail themselves of a kind of legitimate and almost hereditary title for their membership in the dominating class. Therein we may see how the principle of heredity (even if only fictitious) hastens in the highest degree the process of social training, that is, the adaptation of the new forces that emerge in society to the old environment.

If, on the one hand, the nobility shows itself rather favorably disposed to welcome to its bosom those parts of the middle class that seek to raise themselves to their level, on the other hand there is manifest also in the nobility a strong tendency, proceeding from the old spirit of biological caste, to demand the re-establishment of the original purity.

One hears from members of the old nobility frequent loud utterances pleading for a regeneration. Thus in Italy, a person of most ancient aristocratic extraction. Francesco Guasco di Bisio, in his preface to a dictionary of the Piedmontese feudal nobility in several volumes,[37] expresses the opinion that it would be desirable to be able to distinguish, and indeed in the very name itself, whether the noble families had or had not in the past owned a fief, a circumstance which would presume their belonging to the ancient landed nobility. He would ask whether the family be of middle-class origin and had been given the right to a noble title. For often as a result of this practice a feudal name (the name of a town), which remains purely decorative, is added to the bourgeois name, and is permanently retained, so that it may result in bringing about new nobility. This would have happened, it should be said, after 1815 (circa).

To sum up, it should appear from the name itself whether the noble designation represents the survival of a social and juridical status or is only a predicate to the family name. Guasco asks that it be prescribed for instance, that the Marquis L. M. del V. whose ancestors were simply M. and who later obtained the title of Marquis and the predicate "del V." should always bear in his name, as a sign of recognition of his origin, the word M. The name then could be analyzed thus: title, Marquis; name, L.; surname, M.; predicate, del V.[38] Only he whose family name was identical by right with the predicate should belong to the ancient feudal nobility. Guasco maintains that only those families that in olden times exercised the right of jurisdiction should have the prerogative of bearing the name of the fiefs owned by them, annexing it directly to the noble title or to the baptismal name or even, if it pleased them, to both, so that the only noble prerogative now possible, that of a past expressed with unfailing certainty in the name, would not be forgotten. In establishing these principles Guasco operates on a historical presupposition that lays claim to both right and public morality. The privilege of annexing to the given name that of one's former feudal possessions should be understood also as an opportune means of eliminating equivocations and attempts of presumptuous neo-aristocrats to deceive their neighbors.[89] Such vindications emanate from the desire to reconstruct nobility on the basis of the feudal concept.

But such aristocratic selection, however practical from the purely historical point of view, would result, in consequence of the projected reform, in democracy, since by the application of Guasco's proposal the nobility would come out decimated. The great majority of nobles would be deprived of many of their own qualities; they would become, so to say, de-nobled, a cruel fate, such as could not have been wished on the nobility even by the democrats of the eighteenth century.

Still nobility remains the more restricted term, aristocracy the wider. Nobility holds itself at the helm and does not even dream of disappearing from the stage of history. Though not coinciding with aristocracy, and not constituting more than a part of it, nobility gradually takes hold of it and makes itself its master; it pervades, conquers, and molds the high middle class according to its own model and its own needs and imprints on it the seal of its own moral and social essence. Thus the force of attraction of the old dominating class is such as to attain in a short lapse of time the assimilation of all the new participants or aspirants to its power.

THE ELITE AND THE PROLETARIAT

Now we ask ourselves what is the problem of the elite in relation to the position of the proletariat.

Does an elite exist in the proletariat and, if it exists, does it remain in the bosom of the proletariat itself? Experience shows us that there is an elite, but that it does not remain in the proletariat. The educated worker elevates himself from his social stratum. The very fact that he emerges makes him change his social membership. As the superior stratum of the middle class aspires to enter into the nobility in an aristocratic country, so the proletariat aims to form a part of the middle class. It is the "law of imitation" to which Gabriel Tarde refers by which the inferiors move toward the superiors.[40] Anyone may see that the impulse toward social *capillarity* in the proletariat is very strong and clearly evident. As Joly felicitates himself on the elevation instinct of the middle class,[41] so D'Avenel experiences an equal pleasure in ascertaining a similar need in the working classes in regard to the middle class, provided that such elevation remains limited to imitation only.

For D'Avenel "this imitation is the result of liberty, and at the same time is the source of progress of a people." And speaking of peasants who are reproached because they want to make "gentlemen" of their children, he affirms that "a country where the laborers would want their children never to be anything but laborers, would be a country condemned to die."[42] As it was already said in 1842 by the first professor of political economy at the College de France, Michel Chevalier: "One then cannot have an end with the bourgeoisie: one must understand that it embraces each day a new part of the population. . . . The worker to whom you give a public job, if he has the excellence of his post, from that time forward is a bourgeois."[43]

Now here it is not convenient to have any illusions: they are very few, those who, born in the lower strata of society, pass to the superior levels. Research on the origin of illustrious men bears witness to that. By its findings, the proletariat, although numerically preponderant, has given only a very modest percentage to the upper classes and the legend of genius hidden in the attic does not correspond to reality. According to the patient computations of Alfred Odin, 30 per cent of celebrated men come from the official class, 25 per cent from the nobility, 27 per cent from liberal professions, and only 10 per cent from the less wealthy classes.[44] According to the research of Alphonse de Candolle, analysis of the descent of great men shows that 52 per cent are by origin from the liberal professions, 41 per cent from the nobility and the plutocracy, and only 7 per cent from the proletariat.[45]

Are we dealing with organic or only functional inferiority? It is hard to give this difficult question a sufficiently exact answer. The study of the labor movement in all countries, as I believe I have indicated definitely in my historical and statistical studies, shows that the so-called conscious proletariat has allowed and still does allow itself to be led, in its intellectual and political struggles, by outlaws of the middle class. It gives nothing itself to the conduct of its own organizations save a contribution which for quantity and for quality is quite pitiful.[46] However an exception is found to a certain point in the leadership in economic struggles, which have given birth to the formation of groups of labor leaders, well-advanced and bold. And though they and the leaders of industry might show each other their fists, as Einaudi says, fundamentally they feel themselves to be spiritual brothers.[47]

The certainty of being condemned to hired labor throughout natural life is one of the most important causes that lead to the rise of anti-capitalistic movements in the modern masses. The most evident proof of it is that wherever there remains in the workers any hope whatever, founded or unfounded, of approaching emancipation or elevation to the dignity of proprietors, anti-capitalistic movements do not take root or at least do not thrive. So long as free land was to be found in America, wages remained high, since only thus could the contractors hold their workers and avoid the loss of their most productive forces.[48] Wherever in America the frugal worker had a glimpse of the possibility of becoming independent by buying, or even only renting, a farm, the socialist movement did not appear.[49]

As it is now, we cannot hide the evidence that the proletariat, taken as a whole, experiences greater difficulty in elevating itself than in times gone by, since social disparities have become (and certainly because of factory labor) more and more profound. In the initial period of the capitalistic epoch, the cases in which individual workers were successful in ascending to the employer class were fairly frequent. It is affirmed that in northern France, toward 1836, the major part of the industrialists was still of proletarian origin; many had become rich in the first years of the Second Restoration (after 1815). But in the same period, it could already be foreseen that such eventualities would not present themselves in the next generation.[50] D'Avenel thinks he is able to say of recent times that the majority of the leaders of modern French industry, whose names he mentions, have started without capital or at least with only very little.[51] It is not known, however, whether these privileged individuals had been really manual workers.

In England, too, in the first phase of the capitalistic industrial concentration, a large number of employers and inventors were sons of the people. Such were Arkwright, Peel, Strutt, Ashton, Cobden. Herkner thought he saw in the research of Professor Chapman that, even in 1912, the major part of the manufacturers, factory managers, and agents of the spinning and textiles establishments of Lancashire were of proletarian birth.[52] Generally speaking, however, this phenomenon had almost vanished by the end of the first half of the nineteenth century.[53]

In Germany, about twenty years later, Friedrich Albert Lange, after mature researches completed in this field, warned that, although it may be true indeed that the accidents of fortune and speculation always favor some workers to the point of making them employers, nevertheless all the biographies of enriched workers show that they had not succeeded by scraping together small savings by labor done continuously at the same firm and by enlarging them into capital by economy and parsimony.[54]

In America, where industry came to life later, the type of the self-made man still thrives at a time when in Europe he has already almost disappeared. But it is of value to observe that in America the self-made man has not quite always been of proletarian origin. Moreover, even there the type is disappearing, as a direct result of the ever greater development of the trusts.[55]

As for Italy, where heavy industry emerged even later than in America, Einaudi tells us in 1897 that, in the Biella district, the period in which the leaders of industry were still recruited among the self-made men could be said at last to be at an end.[56]

The discouragement of the worker over the general invariability of his own social position was not late in showing itself. In France we see him taken into consideration by Considerant[57] and Proudhon.[58] Even the representatives of the "Social Peace" under Napoleon III could not deny that hired labor had become "l'etat permanent d'une certaine partie de la population."[59]

Contemporaneously, the rich on their side were giving indications of being convinced of the stability of their patrimony. This constituted a complementary phenomenon that made the destiny of the inferior class appear harder yet.[60] Unlimited evils came from it; a few of them are treated generally in this work. We may cite one small indication of social consequences before concluding. A huge part of the workers, even the educated ones, became quite indifferent to their ancestry. From an investigation made in the great Sulzer iron works at Winterthur, Switzerland, it appears that a good fifth of the workers there did not know of any answer to give concerning the profession of their grandfathers.[61]

NOTES

1. Vilfredo Pareto, *Les systèmes socialistes*, Paris: Giard et Brière, 1902, Vol. II.
2. P. E. Fahlbeck, *Sveriges Adel, I. Aetternas Demographi*, Lund, 1898. Also *La Noblesse de Suèdes: Etude demographique*. A Summary by the author is in the *Bulletin de l'Institut International de Statistique*, Vol. XII, No. 1. Oslo: Steen, 1900, pp. 170ff.
3. *Ibid.*, pp. 173–174.
4. *Ibid.*, p. 180.
5. The recent studies of Franco Savorgnan on average families of Germany and Austria from 1890 to 1909 confirm the thesis already sustained by

others that the nobility, in the matter of marriages and birth rate, do not differ markedly from the rest of the population, and even surpass for longevity and genealogical perseverance, and therefore for procreative faculty, the French official class and the rich Americans. It is true that the families he takes as average are found to be on a rather high economic level, which at least shelters them from some of the dangers that threaten other noble families. (Franco Savorgnan, "Das Aussterben der adligen Geschlechter," *Jahrbuch für Soziologie*, Vol. I, Karlsruhe: Braun, 1925, p. 326.)

6. Benoiston de Châteauneuf, *Mémoire statistique sur la durée des Familles Nobles en France*, Paris: Journal d'Hygiene, 1845.

7. Appropriately Furlan says: "Experience teaches generally that the mortality of the elite is notably less than that of the rest of the population, a thing which relates directly to the infant mortality rate which is the principal factor in the general mortality rate. Material well-being and superior education especially determine this difference. For the rest, it must be granted that where the elites retain for themselves the exclusive rights of the military profession, mortality very probably was much higher in the elite than in the rest of the population." (L. V. Furlan, "La circulation des elites," *Revue Internationale de Sociologie*, XIX, No. 6, 1911, p. 389.)

8. *Memoires de M. le Marquis de Fenquières, contenant ses maximes sur la guerre et l'application des exemples aux maximes*, Nouv. Edit., London and Paris: Rollin, 1750, Vol. 1, p. 1.

9. C. Louandre, *Histoire de la noblesse française*, p. 191.

10. Benoiston de Châteauneuf, *loc. cit.*

11. Sigmund Schott, *Alte Mannheimer Familien. Ein Beitrag zur Familien-statistik des XIX. Jahrhunderts*, Mannheim und Leipzig: Bensheimer, 1910, p. 33.

12. *Ibid.*, pp. 21–23.

13. *Ibid.*, p. 32.

14. *Ibid.*, p. 26.

15. Armin Tille in an essay on "Genealogie und Sozialwissenschaft," thinks that about 1700 there could no longer be found in the German cities even a single patrician (*ratsfähige Person*) descending from a patrician of 1600. (*Handbuch der praktischen Genealogie*, Ed. Heydenreich, Leipzig: Degener, 1913, Vol. 1, p. 380.)

16. Schott, *loc. cit.*, p. 66.

17. From Fahlbeck's statistics we find that in Sweden the birth rate of females exceeds that of males thus: in the fourth generation families, the ratio stands at 100 to 79.08 and in those of the sixth generation at 100 to 69.12 (pp. 178ff).

18. Gädke, in *Berliner Tageblatt*, XXXIII, No. 41.

19. F. Funck-Brentano, in *Le National Suisse*, Nov. 20, 1914.

20. *Debrett for 1917*, London: Dean (Cf. *The Daily Mail*, Dec. 15, 1916).

21. Hugh Dalton, *With British Guns in Italy: A Tribute to Italian Achievement*, London: Methuen, 1919, p. 123.

22. Werner Sombart, *Die deutsche Volkswirtschaft im neunzehnten Jahrhundert*, Berlin: Bondi, 1903, p. 542.

23. Giacomo Montalto, *La questione sociale e il partito socialista*, Milano: Soc. Ed. Lomb., 1895, p. 81.

24. Guiseppe Giusti, *Proverbi toscani*, Florence: 1885, p. 171.
25. V. de Lapouge, *Race et milieu social*, Paris: Riviere, 1909, p. 218.
26. Vicomte D'Avenel, *Les Francais de mon temps*, Paris: Nelson, p. 80.
27. Victor Riquetti de Mirabeau, *L'ami des Hommes, ou Traité de la Population*, 4th ed. Hamburg: Herold, 1758, pp. 511–512.
28. So at Cologne. Cf. Edmund Renard, Köln, Leipzig: Seemann, 1907, p. 193.
29. In the Italy of 1700, Ortes ventured, in regard to the *fidei commissa*, the mortmain, the convents, and the celibate class that "the equilibrium of wealth must not be broken by increasing it for some and diminishing it for others. It would be a useless enterprise to destroy them with the vain hope of obtaining that which never has been obtained." (Giuseppe Pecchio, *Storia della Economia Pubblica in Italia*, loc. cit., p. 166.)
30. Werner Wittich, "Der soziale Gehalt von Goethes Roman 'Wilhelm Meisters Lehrjahre' " in *Erinnerungsgabe für Max Weber*, Munich: 1922, Vol. II, pp. 296ff.
31. Jacques Savary, *Le Parfait Négociant*, 6th ed. Lyons: Lyon, 1712, pp. 26–27.
32. René Johannet, *Eloge du bourgeois français*, Paris: Grasset, 1924, p. 159.
33. *Ibid.*, p. 163.
34. Pierre Edouard Lémontey, "Essai sur l'établissement monarchique de Louis XIV," appendix to *Nouveaux Mémoires de Dangeau*, republished by the author, Paris: Deterville, 1818, p. 392.
35. Abbé de Choisy, *Memoires pour servir à l'Histoire de Louis XIV*, Utrecht: Van De Water, 1727, p. 23.
36. Consult the fitting illustrations with which Werner Sombart supports this thesis, *Die deutsche Volkswirtschaft im XIX Jahrhundert*, op. cit., pp. 545ff.
37. Francesco Guasco (Marchese Francesco Guasco di Bisio), *Dizionario feudale degli antichi Stati Sardi e della Lombardia dell' epoca carolingica ai nostri tempi*, Vol. I, Pinerolo: Chiantore e Mascarelli, 1911.
38. Analogy with certain German names such as Heyl von Herrnsheim is suggested.
39. Guasco, *op. cit.*, p. x.
40. Gabriel Tarde, *Les Lois de l'Imitation: Etude Sociologique*, 2nd ed. Paris: Alcan, 1895, p. 282.
41. Henry Joly, *Psychologie des Grands Hommes*, 4th ed., Paris: Ed. "Spes," p. 133.
42. D'Avenel, *op. cit.*, p. 81.
43. Michel Chevalier, *Cours d' Economie politique*, 2nd ed., Paris: Capelle, 1855, Vol. I, p. 160.
44. Alfred Odin, *La genèse des grands hommes*, Paris: 1895.
45. Alphonse de Candolle, *Histoire des sciences et des savants durant deux siècles*, Geneva: 1885.
46. Roberto Michels, *La sociologia del partito politico*, pp. 266–355.
47. Luigi Einaudi, *Le lotte del lavoro*, Turin: Gobetti, 1924, p. 185.
48. This is the famous theory of free land elaborated by a whole series of thinkers, among them Karl Marx (*Das Kapital*. 2nd ed. Hamburg, 1872, Vol. 1, p. 795) and Achille Loria (*La Costituzione economica odierna*, Turin: Bocca, 1899, p. 1 and *passim*).
49. Werner Sombart, *Warum gibt es in den Vereinigten Staaten keinen Sozialismus?* Tübingen: Mohr, 1906, p. 136.

50. Michelet, Le Peuple, p. 55.
51. D'Avenel, op. cit., p. 275.
52. Heinrich Herkner, Die Arbeiterfrage: Eine Einführung, 7th ed., Berlin and Leipzig: Verein Wissenschaftlicher Verleger, 1921, Vol. I, p. 60.
53. John Stuart Mill, Principles of Political Economy, London: Standard edition, p. 503; Léon Faucher, Etudes sur l'Angleterre, Paris: Guillaumin, 1845, p. 156.
54. Friedrich Albert Lange, Die Arbeiterfrage: Ihre Bedeutung für Gegenwart und Zukunft, 3rd ed. Winterthur: Bleuer, 1875, pp. 94, 101. It is true that another German author of the same period holds that "the worker who has an economic education, in sum, he that combines a rare thing—knowledge and technical skills with the qualities of manager and business-man—will find almost always a way to become a contractor in his own right, and therefore independent. Nor will he easily let persons who, in intelligence or in culture are more or less below his level, employ him." (Julius Fröbel, Die Privatwirtschaft und die Volkswirtschaft, Leipzig: Wigand, 1874, p. 128.)
55. Gustavus Myers, History of the Great American Fortunes (German edition: Geschichte der grossen Vermögen in Amerika, Berlin: Fischer, 1916, with preface by Max Schippel) Vol. II, p. 531.
56. Luigi Einaudi, op. cit., p. 27.
57. Victor Considérant, Principes du Socialisme. Manifeste de la démocratie au XIX siècle, Paris: Libr. Phalanst., 1847, p. 5.
58. P. J. Proudhon, La Révolution sociale demontrée par le Coup d'Etat du 2 décembre, Brussels: Riessling, 1852, p. 19; Lorenz Von Stein, Volkswirtschaftslehre, 2nd ed., Vienna: Braumüller, 1878, pp. 524ff.
59. Henri Baudrillart, Le Salariat et l'Association (Conférences populaires sous le Patronage de S. M. l'Impératrice), Paris: Hachette, 1867, p. 26.
60. "Generally, being born means, inevitably, entering a certain social class, nor is it easy afterward to come out of it." Michael Hainisch, Der Kampf ums Dasein und die Sozialpolitik, Leipzig and Vienna: Deuticke, 1899, p. 40.
61. Ernst Bernheim, Auslese und Anpassung (Berufswahl und Berufsschicksal) der Arbeiterschaft in der Heizungsfabrik von Gebr. Sulzer A. G. Ober-winterthur [Degree Thesis, Zurich, 1916] Bern: 1916, p. 77).

CHAPTER IV

Democratic and Aristocratic Tendencies in Modern Politics

THE EMERGENCE OF THE MASS FACTOR IN POLITICS

THE history of the nineteenth century was symbolized by universal suffrage. For the suffragists, the extension of this right represented the peak value of the century and gave tangible proof of the right of all, including the substantial illiterate portions of some countries, to participate, at least legally and abstractly, in parliamentary elections, and thus in public affairs. This guarantee was wrested, in part forcibly, from the middle classes by the property-less in the ingenuous belief that it would be a panacea capable of healing all their real or pretended sufferings. Yet Mosca is also right when he speaks of the granting of the suffrage as a concession of the ruling classes. For in some countries the ruling groups evidenced weariness and indecision, imbued as they were with the prevailing doctrines of eighteenth-century politics as transmitted to the nineteenth century. According to these doctrines, the only legitimate government was one based on popular sovereignty, the numerical majority of the political community.[1]

Many other motives contributed to the irresistible movement that brought the suffrage to all citizens of voting age. Mosca points out that, by conceding the vote, the ruling-class minority, while neither relinquishing nor intending to relinquish its grip, could ease its burning conscience and avoid the accusation of inconsistency of principles which threatened not only its conscience but (we may add) its power as well.

88

Other considerations are found in other countries. In Prussia, universal suffrage was derived from the dissensions that rent the middle classes around 1860. It is a well-documented fact that Bismarck, creator of the popular electorate, accepted Lassalle's advice to give the vote to the young working class, so that with its help and that of the nobility the petulant and radical middle classes might be controlled. For he wrongly and strangely believed the bourgeoisie dangerous to the monarchy.[2]

In Italy, as in other countries, the enlargement of the electorate came from a mixture of sentiments of gratitude toward the people who fought a war and of hasty resort to prophylaxis against the Bolshevist threat immediately following the war. Thus the masses ascended to the parliamentary stage in the persons of their delegates. And so a great popular superstition found its basis. As Spencer stated it so efficaciously: "The great political superstition of the past was the divine right of kings; the great superstition of the present is the divine right of parliaments. The anointing oil seems unawares to have dripped from the head of the one on to the heads of the many and gives sacredness to them also and to their decrees."[3]

Long before Spencer, spectator of the democratic tragicomedy of nineteenth-century England, the gist of the matter was related by an eighteenth-century French thinker who lived before the rise of democratic institutions and to whom impartial history accredits the fatherhood of democracy itself. This was Rousseau, and he says: "To take the term in its fully rigorous meaning, there has never existed a true democracy and one will never exist. It is against the natural order of things that the great number governs and that the small number be governed."[4]

We also call to mind Kant's statement: "Of the three forms of government, the democratic form, in the real meaning of the word, is necessarily a despotism, because it establishes an executive power; for the "all" which is not really the all decides concerning, and sometimes against, the one who has not participated in the decision. The general will is a contradiction to itself and to freedom."[5]

Today the concept of democracy finds itself in a state of deterioration at the hands of historical events. In Italy democracy at first approved vociferously the Fascist march on Rome. Then suddenly, a *posteriori*, it disapproved it, not because the new regime seemed illegal in its origins (that had been applauded and condoned),[6] not because of its intrinsic theoretical principles, but because its extra-legality was lasting "too long." The chief dissent of Italian democracy from Fascism was not juridical, nor logical, but "chronological" in character.

Max Weber, almost unequalled in understanding among the men Germany has produced in the last half century—a jurist and economist, sociologist, philosopher, musician, man of affairs, and chief theorist of the dawning democracy of postwar Germany—was asked by General Ludendorff what he meant by the term "democracy." He answered that democracy was a political system in which the people elect a leader whom they can trust, whereupon, this accomplished, the elected one obtains the right to impose on people and parties the most absolute silence. Nor might such a leader again be censured or condemned unless he committed grave errors.[7]

In Austria Baron von Wieser, liberal minister in the last cabinet of the declining monarchy as well as the last survivor of the so-called "Marginal Utility" school, occupying thereby an eminent place in the contemporary history of economic doctrine, wrote his final work on the concept of political power. In it he unhesitatingly advances the thesis that the violation of public constitutional law may be considered as democratic provided that after the illegal act the transgressor obtains from his people their retrospective approval, convinced meanwhile of the political necessity for the relative illegality. Accordingly, Wieser feels that Bismarck was justified in ignoring a contrary vote of the Prussian diet and making great expenditures for the army. And Benito

Mussolini, maintains Wieser, is not an enemy of democracy, but an enemy of its faults and defectiveness.[8]

Still a second bitter delusion awaited the masses at the crossroads of modern history, and this one was purely of Marxist origin. Marxism, with its apocalyptic theories of capitalistic concentration, of growing misery, and of final catastrophe, filled the minds of millions of workers of all lands with a false sense of security in their inescapable triumph. It did this first to the socialist organizations,[9] providing an enormous stimulus to their fighting spirit, and giving them a supreme consolation in that they were not to be the pariahs of all present and future societies but rather the next and glorious heirs of the world. The dogma from which so-called scientific socialism had fashioned its worker battalions and which had filled so many small brains with doctrinaire pretensions, brought about the strengthening of its mortal enemy in an unexpected way. There can be no denying, indeed, the important consequences of the Marxist dogma that capitalism and industry will concentrate increasingly, and that this period of monopoly will be the indispensable transition between the era of proletarian suffering and the future society.

Its application in democratic, elective form has been the well-known slogan, dear to the Socialist demagogues of Italy, Germany, and France: "Through Capitalism to Socialism!" Indoctrinated with it, the industrial workers and their instructed representatives followed a legislative, social, and commercial policy in nearly every respect favorable to large-scale industry and prejudicial to the interests of the middle classes. For Marxian theory held the bourgeoisie to be the remnants of the past, bound to disappear, or even better to be dross whose rapid elimination would render easier the triumphal march of the labor army toward its coveted and predicted goal.

Therefore, it is no mere paradox to affirm with Kurt Suckert that French, German, English, and American capitalism (and we may add that of upper Italy) could never have reached its formidable power position if it had not been supported by socialism, which, by disciplining the proletariat to obey orders and by transforming the handicrafts spirit into a corporate one, operated against its own law.[10]

THE FORMATION OF THE ECONOMIC ELITE

Wealth is a means of acquiring power. For many men wealth constitutes principally an indispensable means of attaining social aims of a non-economic nature. Money loses its value except as it may satisfy the "voluptuousness" of ruling over their fellow men. English philosophy of the seventeenth century was pervaded by this notion that the human race was congenitally addicted to the "instinct of power" (Hobbes) and to "self-love" and the "instinct of sovereignty" (Mandeville).[11] Such an instinct would lead each human being to aim above everything else at forcing persons and things to submit to his will. There is, in fact, according to Genovesi (1820), a psychological law derived from experience, to the effect that we men, not being able "to receive any great pleasure if others consent to our will, nor any great displeasure if they oppose us, strive to rule over men to demonstrate the ability and force of the body, or spiritual force, or for the splendor of civil life. One recognizes that men may become in some part masters of others in all three ways. And firstly, in respect to physical force, this is what binds the conquerors to the conquered. Secondly is the force of ingenuity, that which the wise use with respect to the ignorant and the shrewd with respect to the foolish. The third, finally, is the splendor and luxury of civil life by which the great and the rich through the pomp of living dominate those who cannot afford to behave similarly."[12]

From the time of Genovesi to the present the thirst for power has not changed. Or at most it has changed the form in which it is manifested. In the seventeenth century the happiness of the wealthy man was formed of the admiration surrounding him because of his splendor and reckless royalty. In the age of capitalism, supported by democracy, the rich man is happy whenever his money can give him great influence over his economic inferiors and over public affairs. It thus begins with ambition but aims at glory. "The perfect merchant," said Rubichon when modern capitalism was still in its infancy, "is composed of two imperfections: he exhibits great avarice and great ambition."[13] Certainly the instinct of power can be satisfied within the area of economics through a great intensification of the power of command. Therefore, if we may have faith in persons competent in these matters, it seems that in the development of the bargaining or merchant type much more ambition than avarice is required.[14]

Biographical studies that speak of the lives of our contemporary plutocrats demonstrate how much of the dynamic force of great industrialists and merchants, directed at reaching the pinnacle of wealth, is basically subordinated to the end of acquiring authority over men and establishing themselves as autocrats of finance. The zeal and conscientious application to work, the capacity and pertinacity in trading are but accessories even in all their greatness. The long duration and limitless extent of their industriousness and of their eagerness for profit, often outdoing the limitations of their age, are subordinated to the object of arriving. Carnegie asserts that he would not give a cent for a clerk who did not dream from the first moment of his employment by a firm of becoming a partner in it or its owner.[15] Carnegie himself tells us that from his youth his one thought has always been that of becoming an owner, of thereby producing a large output of goods, and of giving work to many people.[16] Such words embody in their apparent modesty the half-concealed desire for domination. Nathan Rothschild expressed a similar thought in his advice to young merchants, "To give mind and soul and heart and body, everything to business, because that is the way to be happy."[17]

A leading English economist, Marshall, unhesitatingly ad-

vances the thesis that "the chief motive to the highest constructive work in industry is a chivalrous desire to master
difficulties and obtain recognized leadership."[18] The coal king
in America is described to us as a righteous autocrat with
megalomanic tendencies, "cruel as the grave."[19] This psychology is not a monopoly of England and North America.
In France Schneider de Le Creusot is presented to us as a
"beneficent and authoritarian person, an absolute monarch."[20]

For Italy Einaudi has analyzed in the Italo-American Dell
'Acqua a closely similar type. Dell 'Acqua also was an autocrat who gives orders and who has his "well-organized kingdom." He commands an army "which moves compactly under
the supreme direction of a general who has conducted it to
victory through many battles against almost insuperable obstacles and the terrible assaults of adverse fortune."[21] In Germany the great industrialist and physicist Werner Siemens
never cared to accept the title of Knight of Labor (*Kommer-
zienrat*) offered to him by the government, asserting that
such a title was not applicable to the social function which
he performed. In the end he accepted with great personal
satisfaction the title of *Regierungsrat*, Councillor of State, a
title which seemed more congruous with his social position,
"because the great industrialist is a public personage invested
with quasi-official character and therefore a title well befits
him which denotes, even if only in a figurative sense, duties
conforming to the government of public affairs."[22]

Young Siemens, to whom Germany owes a great part of its
electrical industry, candidly confesses that in business his only
stimulus was ambition.[23] Of the two giants of the German
metallurgic industry, Thyssen and Stinnes, a competent judge
in the matter asserts enthusiastically that "they hold in
small consideration the purely routine efforts of their manual
worker," but that they themselves are the real workers for
whom the day of work has "twenty-five" hours, and that in
their fierce zeal they contemptuously decline titles that could
not but lessen the grandeur of their economic empire.[24] For

another great German entrepreneur, Rathenau, the essential attraction of an enterprise consists in its furnishing to the businessman the possibility of acquiring power, of exerting a great influence "not without, it is true, terrible responsibilities."[25]

The phenomenon of the transference of ability and intellectual capacity may occur even among industrialists. In Germany the ruling houses in industry are not very young. The Siemens family is in its fifth generation. Emil Rathenau was not quite a parvenu.[26] Hugo Stinnes, however, was the nephew of Mathias.[27]

The work of the leaders of industry has been extolled by many and vilified by many others. A great part of the relevant literature bears the stigma of political passion, as, for example, the work of the American Myers on the genesis of the great American fortunes of today.

The formation of such an elite has not only given rise to a distinct kind of plutocratic authority, but has also in a high degree influenced the conduct of the World War. During the war, the great leaders of industry directed important departments, particularly technical and economical ones, since such commitments require a solid competence which is not acquired without practice in vast private affairs.[28] In France a young assistant secretary of state, Georges Bonnet, in a book entitled *Letters of a Young Bourgeois of 1914*, tried to inculcate in his fellow citizens the conviction that it is necessary to substitute in the direction of public affairs, as far as possible, young leadership for old, so as to rejuvenate the machinery of the state, especially that of industry and commerce. This he proposed on the basis of the principles of sixteenth-century French philosophy, especially those of Montaigne, who brought to light the fact that the reputation of great men is often destroyed by their unhappy habitual disposition to stay firmly attached to power for a long time.

Bonnet concludes that it is now the law of political necessity that the young should be gradually admitted into the sanctuaries of economic and social organization. The World War revealed in the bravery of the young, who fought and won it, a new practical basis for consolidation.[29] Even in Germany, defeated and broken, there appear now some attempts at reorganization of commercial life, with the intention of ridding commerce and industry of incompetents and trying to introduce young forces into them.

The formation of the economic elite proceeds truly a little casually and at the mercy of events, and therefore has grave defects, for which it may be rightly criticized. For hereditary rights, conservative mental habits, and other efficient causes, as such, do not act at all in the desired sense of selecting the constructive elements of ownership as a class. It may be well understood how, soon after the war, the stimulus of impelling needs fostered the rise of the neo-Saint-Simonian school in France. To it belonged brilliant names such as Gabriel Darquet, Ferdinand Gros, Francis Delaisi, and others, who above all aimed at the reorganization not so much of the social order, which instead they intended to leave intact, as the "renouveau" of the human element managing the national economy. This new current shared the idea advanced by Saint-Simon at the beginning of the last century that the working class and the industrialist class, together with the technicians and intellectuals, formed after all only one class, which Saint-Simon called "the productive class." This class takes the responsibility for the mass of indispensable labor on behalf of social welfare, and it presents a single psychological type.

Besides Saint-Simon, this new French industrial current appears to be influenced and inspired by the American-made doctrines of Taylor and is impressed by the need for partial application of them. In fact Taylorism aims at valorizing to the utmost (with "motion studies" and with all kinds of instruments able to measure the forces and particular capacity of each worker) the congenital and acquired qualities of the "economic man." Taking the individual's urge to profit as the incentive, Taylorism seeks to minimize losses of time and exploit the full qualities of each single worker. But the neo-Saint-Simonists of France in their review *Le Producteur* pointed out the driving necessity to utilize similar principles in renewing the whole capitalistic class also. This was to be accomplished by the elimination of the unfit and the implacable application of the English maxim "the right man in the right place." That is, even in the owning and managerial class, each qualified person should be placed in the most appropriate position.

Taking up this thread again, the chief of French syndicalistic fascism, Georges Valois, believed that in the regime of the technical masters the incompetent businessman could not, by himself alone, by the strength of things, remain long at the head of an enterprise. He also points out the grave inconvenience that exists in the lack of an institution superior to the managers themselves. He sees the solution in so organizing economic life as to allow a central power to exert pressure on the managers to increase technical efficiency, economic expansion, and the application of new technical methods. According to Valois the action from above would have to be directed mostly against three tendencies, represented by three respective types of masters: (1) he who "bears" the deterioration of economic production by willingly resigning himself to the reduction of his own profits and by putting in some of his own money; (2) he who tries to keep intact his industrial profits, but reduces the remuneration due to labor; and (3) he who grants, indeed, wage increases but who in return transfers the burden to the consumers by increasing the sale price of his products. These three types, unable to solve the cost of production problems, should (still according to Valois) either be induced to seek and find new methods, or disappear.[30] Thus, for example, Francis Delaisi, an economist of the same school, in one of his popular and influential writings, reproached the French petroleum capitalists for being merely profit-greedy bourgeoisie, haters of risks, devoid of energy and of a feeling of responsibility. Those who "hold

the wealth of the nation, ought to contribute to its greatness."[31]

Taylor himself already had conceived industry as a form of
military organization and thought the chief of the firm was
responsible for the progress of the concern.[32] In France Wilbois, a disciple of Bergson, who had opened a school in 1913,
the "Ecole nouvelle," introduced into its program a detailed
test for the essential attitudes of the leader of industry. Here
are the essential qualities that were tested: first, the creative
attitudes, which include, (a) ability at documentation (for
example, the ability to reduce to twenty lines a fifty-page
script, or that of briefly describing a factory after visiting it),
(b) the scientific spirit, (c) the positive spirit, (d) the spirit
of invention; second, attitudes of dominance, divided into
two sub-categories: (a) dominant attitudes whose field of
action is found outside of human contact such as the spirit
of foresight, of initiative, of organization, and of control, and
(b) dominant attitudes of direct applicability in contact with
persons, as the faculty of recruitment and of education, of
manual labor, that of command, that of coordination. Finally,
the examinations test three more qualifications, the possession
of which gives the right to the so-called "diplome de sortie":
the ability to make decisions, firmness of character, and moral
superiority.[33]

As required by their aims, the neo-Saint-Simonists do not
hesitate even to chip away, although with due caution, at
hereditary rights. Though admitting that inheritance corresponds to an invincible tendency of human nature, such a
right may constitute in certain circumscribed cases an ob-
stacle to the free mobility of the elite. It tends to act as a
handicap to those who inherit nothing except some moral
virtues that are of little monetary value.[34] The new industrial
school, even on this point, ties itself to the genuine ideas of
Saint-Simon, who deemed initial equality necessary for the
development of humanity, that which Anglo-American economists call "equality of opportunity."

The same principles are supposed to apply also to the intellectuals employed by industry. Enfantin was a leader in this respect. He was indignant at the unjust treatment of the intellectuals by modern society. They earn less than a railroad man, "whose work consists of lubricating the wheels of the locomotive."[35] The neo-Saint-Simonists did their utmost to devise means adequate to remedy the injustice and make the most select and endowed part of the intellectuals capable of rising little by little to the dignity of leaders of industry. And so they conceived the project of creating certain banks which were to be directed by the producers, that is, the "disinterested creators who can treat money as a slave." They also proposed to create an insurance and credit system to fill an unfortunate gap in the system of Saint-Simon. "Yes indeed," shouts Gilbert Maire, "the new technical institutions of credit are to provide assurances of the future to the inventive elite who are deprived of inheritances. Creative activities, today ignored by the banks, will possess their instruments of creation; in short, advancing the necessary capital is less important than initiative of recognized quality, be it managerial, intellectual, or operational. Oh yes, I say that such institutions have within them what it takes to resolve the crisis of inheritance."[36] The passage of capable workers and clerks to the immediate management of industry thus will be facilitated. Wilbois' program "tends to unite all producers who desire mutually to increase and revaluate production by means of young leaders and directors, men who have achieved success and the young who wish to arrive."[37]

Fundamentally, all these tendencies aim at but one thing, in itself impossible, but worthy just the same for its high educative value; that is, to do away, in matters of capital, with the capitalist who would be but a means to the end, an instrument, not an object in himself. It would be the same as rationalizing capitalism.[38] There is no doubt that, in Italy, even fascism entertains some idea not dissimilar to that which we have outlined here.[39]

NOTES

1. Gaetano Mosca, *Elementi di Scienza Politica*, 2nd ed., Turin: Bocca, 1923, p. 480.
2. Bismarck, *Gedanken und Erinnerungen*, Stuttgart: Cotta, 1898.
3. Herbert Spencer, *The Man versus the State*, London: Watts, 1914, p. 66.
4. Jean Jacques Rousseau, *Contrat Social*.
5. Kant, quoted in Ottokar Lorenz, *Die Geschichtswissenschaft in Hauptrichtungen und Aufgaben, kritisch erörtert*, Berlin: Hertz, 1886, p. 63.
6. Quintino Piras, *Battaglie liberali*, Novara: Tip. Gaddi, 1926, p. 16.
7. Marianne Weber, *Max Weber, Ein Lebensbild*, Tubingen: Mohr, 1926, p. 429.
8. Friedrich Wieser, *Das Gesetz der Macht*, Vienna: Springer, 1926, p. 520.
9. At this point I would remind the reader of my books: *La Teoria di C. Marx sulla miseria crescente e le sue origine*, Turin: Bocca, 1922, and *Psychologie der antikapitalistischen Massenbewegungen*, in *Grundriss der Sozialökonomik*, X, No. 1. Tübingen: Mohr, 1924.
10. Curzio Suckert, *L'Europa vivente. Teoria storica del sindacalisms nazionale*, Florence: Voce, 1923, p. 43.
11. Bernard de Mandeville, *An Inquiry into the Origin of Honour*, London, 1732, p. 43.
12. Genovesi, *op. cit.*, Vol. II, p. 292.
13. M. Rubichon, *Du Mécanisme de la Société en France et en Angleterre*, Nouv. Ed., Paris, 1837, p. 215.
14. Werner Sombart, *Der Bourgeois*, pp. 121–213. In the celebrated drama of Octave Mirbeau, "Les Affaires sont les affaires," which may be translated as "Business is business," the salient traits of a merchant type center around his boundless ambition. "The ambitions of Lechat are limitless. . . . Pitiless towards the humble, ferocious towards those who resist him, he piles ruin upon ruin about him for the sake of personal profit. He precipitates bankruptcies, drives men to suicide, and passes through life like a predatory beast . . . In the business world he is nicknamed Lechat-Tigre! A name that flatters him and of which he is even proud."
15. Andrew Carnegie, *Empire of Business*, New York, 1902, p. 2. But Carnegie, so speaking, only repeated under the form of postulate that which, unknown to him, Tocqueville had related a century before as "matter of fact" of American life (see *La democratie en Amerique*, Vol. I, Part II, p. 207).
16. Carnegie, *Autobiography*, p. xvi.
17. H. R. Bourne, *Life of Buxton, English Merchant*, London, 1886 (2nd ed.), p. 465.
18. Alfred Marshall, "Economic Chivalry," in the *Economic Journal*, Vol. XVII, No. 65 (March, 1907), p. 14.
19. Henry Demarest Lloyd, *Lords of Industry*, New York-London: Putnam, 1910, p. 265. Also Gustavus Myers, *Geschichte der grossen amerikanischen Vermögen* (German Edit., Vol. II) which contains a minute analysis, though somewhat superficial and exaggerated, of the spoliative character of private American wealth.
20. Vicomte G. D'Avenel, *Le Mécanisme de la vie moderne*, Paris: Colin, 1908, Vol. I, p. 151.

21. Luigi Einaudi, *Un principe mercante: Studio sulla espansione commerciale italiana*, Turin: Bocca, 1900, pp. 19, 159, etc.

22. Kurt Wiedenfeld, *Das Persönliche im modernen Unternehmertum*, p. 60; also Adolph Goetz, *Ballin, der Königliche Kaufmann*, 4th ed., Leipzig: Seemann, 1907, p. 76.

23. Siemens, *Letter to his brother Carl*, 1867, Thunen Archiv, edited by Richard Ehrenberg, Vol. I (1906), p. 313.

24. Les Jolles, "Stinnes," in *Kapitalanlage und Geldmarkt, Der Tag*, March 24, 1910 (supplement); cf. also Hermann Brinckmeyer, *Hugo Stinnes*, Munich: Wieland, 1922; Friedrich Beckmann, *Der Zusammenschluss in der westdeutschen Grossindustrie*, Cologne, 1921; Herbert von Beckerath, *Ziele und Gestaltung in der deutschen Industriewirtschaft*, Jena, 1922; Richard Ehrenberg, *Die Unternehmungen der Brüder Siemens*, Jena, 1906; Fr. Fasolt, *Die sieben grössten deutschen Elektrizitätsgesellschaften*, Dresden, 1904; Wilhelm Goetzke, *Das Rheinisch-Westfälische Kohlensyndikat*, Essen, 1905; Curt Goldschmidt, *Ueber die Konzentration im deutschen Kohlenbergbau*, Karlsruhe, 1912; Georg Gradnauer, *Die deutsche Volkswirtschaft*, Berlin, 1921; Kurt Heinig, *Stinnes und seine 600.000 Arbeiter*, Berlin, 1921; J. Kollmann, *Der deutsche Stahlwerksverband*, Berlin; Waldemar Koch, *Die Konzentrationsbewegung in der deutschen Elektroindustrie*, Munich, 1907; Robert Liefmann, *Kartelle und Trusts*, Stuttgart, 1922; K. Schmitz, *Die Verstaatlichung der Schwerindustrie*, Duisburg, 1921; J. Singer, *Das Land der Monopole, Amerika oder Deutschland*, Berlin, 1913; Walter Thoenes, *Die Zwangssyndikate im Kohlenbergbau*, Jena, 1921; Kurt Wiedenfeld, *Das Rheinisch-Westfälische Kohlensyndikat*, Bonn, 1912; Kurt Wiedenfeld, *Ein Jahrhundert rheinischer Montanindustrie*, Bonn, 1915; Paul Ufermann and Carl Hüglin, *Die A. E. G., Eine Darstellung des Konzerns der Allgemeinen Elektrizitäts-Gesellschaft*, Berlin: Verlag für Sozialwissenschaft, 1922.

25. Walter Rathenau, *Reflexionen*, Leipzig: Hirzel, 1908, p. 82.

26. Brinckmeyer, *op. cit.*, p. 16.

27. Ufermann, *op. cit.*, p. 18.

28. Cf. *Revue de Paris*, 1ᵉʳ Janvier 1918, "Lettres sur la Réforme gouvernementale," cited from Jean Vergeot, *Le crédit comme stimulant et régulateur de l'industrie: La Conception Saint-Simonienne, ses réalisations, son application au problème bancaire d'après-guerre*, Paris: Jouve, 1918, p. 11.

29. Georges Bonnet, *Lettres d'un bourgeois de 1914*, Paris: Payot, 1919, pp. 37–47.

30. Georges Valois, *L'économie Nouvelle: L'intelligence et la production, Economie, Morale, Religion*, ed. définitive, Paris: Nouv. Libre. Nationale, 1924, pp. 227–228.

31. Francis Delaisi, "La politique du pétrole," *Le Producteur*, I, 3 (1920), p. 417; also by the same author, *Le pétrole*, Paris: Payot, 1920.

32. Taylor, *Principes d'organisation scientifique des usines*, Paris: Dunod; Taylor, *La Direction des Ateliers*.

33. Marius Andre, "La formation des chefs d'industrie," *Le Producteur*, II, 5 (1920), p. 300.

34. Gabriel Darquet, "Notre Doctrine," *Le Producteur*, IV, 10 (1921), p. 22.

35. Henry Clouard, "L'actualité des Saint-Simoniens," *Le Producteur*, I, 2 (1920), pp. 195–196.

36. Gilbert Maire, "Education et production. I. L'Héritage," *Le Producteur*, II, 1 (1920), p. 68; J. B. Vergeot, *op. cit.*; F. Gros, *L'Assurance: Son sens historique et social*, Paris: Bureau d'Organisation Economique, 1920.

37. Marius André, *op. cit.*, p. 306; and especially J. Wilbois, *Devoir et Durée, Essai de Morale Sociale*, Paris: Alcan, 1912.

38. Benito Mussolini, *La nuova politica dell'Italia: Discorsi e dichiarazioni*, ed. by Amedeo Giannini, Milan: Imperia, 1903, p. 19.

39. It is worthwhile, however, to observe that if it is inhumanly conceived, this ideal may open the door to all kinds of attitudes ranging from the heroic to the foolish. A French writer Hamp, has used it as a subject in one of his comedies. Here is some reasoning: "If I were to quit my position without being certain that he who succeded me here wished better of it than myself, I would be a criminal toward you, toward the factory, and toward my conscience. . . . No concern with profit keeps me here. I would pay to be a worker here." (Pierre Hamp, "La Maison avant tout," in *la Petite Illustration*, No. 166 [1923].)

CHAPTER V

Social Metabolism and Postwar Events

CHANGES in the social class of individuals in a capitalistic order rest on three basic factors: (a) their relationships to the economic and productive process, (b) the fecundity of the various social and occupational groups, and (c) the dynamics of mobility.[1]

The second factor is important in social change in that occupational groups that are not prolific tend to become exogenous. They lose the capacity to recruit their needed functional adherents from among their own stock and occupation. The classes with a higher and less-controlled birth rate, unless deficient in ambitions to rise, are endogenous; they not only replenish the ranks of their own class, but also invade the other classes, particularly those on a higher level. The intellectuals are exogenous,[2] the country folk endogenous.

To state that men seek to better their lot in society by climbing the social ladder is a commonplace.[3] Parents subject themselves to infernal agonies to assure their children an easier future, particularly by helping them achieve a station in life of greater prestige than that to which they once belonged. The very neo-Malthusianism of the birth-control practices in the wealthy classes may even constitute an aspect of this phenomenon. To Pareto, the possibility of rising socially would be diminished if the middle class were so prolific as to take onto itself all the available positions, blocking the entry to them of those born in other classes.[4] The instinct that impels men to retain the powers of government in the hands of their families, transmitting them wherever possible only to their own descendants is so strong that every elective ruler tends to transform himself into a hereditary monarch. Where he is prevented from having natural children, as the Pope, he resorts to substitutes; this apparently was the origin of pontifical nepotism.[5] The neo-Malthusianism of the middle class and of the dominant classes in general constitutes then a safety valve to ensure adequate social mobility.

To the current of middle-class people of modest circumstances moving toward the wealthier and dominant classes is added a converse current of the rich descending toward lower levels. Experience teaches that, numerically, this latter movement is much smaller than the first. The rich may become impoverished, their incomes may be reduced, and some of their number may lose their well-paid positions in the state or in industry. But for most of them, their descent is halted at some intermediary level; they do not move to the very bottom. Whereas one may see persons once rich and powerful, or their descendants, occupying positions well below their former splendid rank, it is quite rare to see them transformed into machine or manual workers.[6]

Many families of the old aristocracy disappear into the masses, as we have indicated above. Inattentive historians have let pass this phenomenon, allowing us to believe that noble families no longer circulating among the aristocracy have become extinct, whereas, as a matter of fact, they have only disappeared from the superficial world of high society.[7] Especially in the Latin countries, impoverished families find their old tenor of life impossible and must adapt themselves to changed conditions. Not infrequently, members of such families go "underground" for a time until they have acquired a new profession, and with it, the means appropriate to their former social status. As long as they remained of the nobility, they could not undertake the professions in question.

Vilfredo Pareto visualized the social process as an enormous machine in action producing continuously, though imperceptibly, new human material destined to regenerate a tired and demoralized world. The vivid and profound meaning of the theory of the circulation of elites rests in his thesis of the perennial renovation of human society by means of the continual rise of persons of the lower and middle classes and their entrance into the ruling class to replace the older families who are condemned to physical and psychic sterility. As I have indicated earlier, however, the old ruling class is not eliminated by the new group, but rather there occurs an amalgamation or fusion.

It is an advantage of democracy to have built its institutions in a way that expands greatly the opportunities for the selection of members of the elite. Democracy thus facilitates exchange of personnel among the social classes.[8] This advantage is a true one, logically indisputable.[9] Of course, other forms of government also operate and prosper by means of a gradual transfusion of new blood into the veins of the top hierarchy. Under Louis XIV of France, Colbert's policy was to ennoble and appoint the most active and capable members of the bourgeoisie to high offices in the state, Napoleon I, in his turn, by placing the baton of a field marshal in the knapsack of every soldier, created the possibility of the birth of an entirely new ruling class.

History teaches that an aristocracy whose ranks are hermetically sealed, rather than attaining stability and permanence, is seriously damaged. No enlightened aristocracy has ever set itself against the laws of social metabolism.

In oligarchic parties, captaincy tends to become a principle; charisma encourages the continual election and re-election of the delegates of the masses. Even in democratic countries and among democratic parties that deny messianic leadership, a directorate of chiefs exists, although democracy formally tries to hide this effective process. The rapid exchange of places among the leaders deceives the inexpert as to the real character of power. It follows that the masses are not the ones who ruin the leaders, but new leaders who use the masses to such ends.

It is true that democracy furnishes to the leading class a larger number of leaders of middle-class origins than aristocracy does. It would be erroneous, however, to suppose that such recruitment means that the whole people have escaped from the power of leaders. The "popular leader" means democracy in the same sense in which, in the field of economics, "the self-made man" means the advent of socialism.

The law of the circulation of the elites destroys the thesis of the possibility of a society without social levels. Political theory and practice have demonstrated that, whatever be the form of government of public affairs, it is always—to repeat again the words of Jean Jacques Rousseau—against the natural order of things that the majority rule and the minority be ruled. It is therefore necessary that the historian and economist insist on the permanence of that factor that Mosca has called the "political class," a term which makes an abstraction of certain moral qualities, which may or may not exist, but which also assumes the existence of capacity, will, and force.

On the other hand, the law of the circulation of the elites destroys equally the supposition of a ruling class that remains closed and inaccessible. There emerges from this theory no vain quietism capable of paralyzing the flights of dynamic idealism nor is it conducive to a philosophy of history summed up in the idea that all movement is hopeless. And in fact, how could the spectacle of the multiform esthetic and ethical forces, even though minoritarian, striving to rule destiny with or without the consent of the multitude, ever be considered fruitless?

THE ELEMENTS OF THE POLITICAL CLASS

Certain reliable indications exist that the science of political class is divided into three camps, corresponding to the three sectors that compose it: the first is political in the sense of energetic volition, the second is economic, and the third is intellectual, working with words, symbols, and science. These three groups together constitute the political class, and their interdependence and interaction are such as to obscure often the criteria that distinguish them from one another. They form circles which, though far from coinciding with one another, have points of intersection. To fix the relations of these circles is the most important and most arduous task before us. Of the roads that lead to social success and to the entrance of new elements into the political class, those which are most direct and rapid are wealth and political dynamism. The question then arises as to what may be the logical and sociological connections among the given constituent elements of the political class as a whole.

It is worth mentioning that, with the rise of the socialist movement, the problem as here stated risked losing all importance. For that movement believed that the government of a nation was nothing else but an exponent of the parallelogram of economic forces. Rather than determining political affairs, the main *subject* is itself the very *object* dominated by economic influence. Pisacane (1855), the first to pose the problem in Italy and one of the propagators of the doctrine elsewhere, declared that political questions vanish in the face of economics: "So long as there will be men who sell themselves out of poverty, government will be the prisoner of the owning class."[10] With this belief, Pisacane stands in marked opposition to the "social democratic" and Mazzinian current, but agrees with Proudhon, who had since 1848 been subjecting the state socialists like Louis Blanc to severe criticism.[11]

Following the theory of Marx, the state is of necessity an instrument in the hands of the class that is the strongest economically. It is a class state (*Klassenstaat*) and in particular a bourgeois state.[12] The followers of Marx have not hesitated to coin an even more impolite term for the state, describing it as "the Executive Committee of the Owning Classes," constituted to defend the interests and privileges of the existing order.[13]

The Marxist thesis of the perfect coincidence of the political class with the highest level of wealth does not escape mauling at the hands of history, however. The social groups that are economically most powerful are not in fact identical with the political class that holds the high offices of the state, and the political class is not inevitably the servant of its will. In the eighteenth century, the French middle class had already achieved financial power, while politically it was subject to the upper classes of the clergy and nobility. Marquis de Mirabeau refers to the fact that the possessions of the third estate were superior to those of the old nobility of the time. The "meat salesman," a coarse figure, displayed a pomp more remarkable than the authentic gentleman. The cause of this phenomenon was the fact that the old dominant classes, especially the military and the judiciary (among whom nobles abounded), had "no right to the sources of money," and could not possess any more than the king deigned to give them in the form of a salary. But the new classes were in a position to exploit fully their fervid activities in the field of business.[14]

There is a historical school that views the advent of the French Revolution precisely as a result of the functional necessity to achieve an equilibrium between these two disparate phenomena. Did not the Revolution have as its task the conferring of political power on those who stood waiting with superior resources, since power must be accompanied by wealth?[15] Yet such a transformation of power was not thereupon consolidated, not even in the chain of events provoked by the subsequent constitutional monarchies. As in Germany also before the war, the bourgeoisie entered into the state for their tax rates, while the nobility instead for political ascendancy.[16]

The Marxist thesis of the identity between the economic and political class does not, therefore, express the whole truth of historical analysis. Our own studies convince us that the leading economic groups maintain always a rather distant relationship to political power. They are not accustomed to take part in decisions on public affairs, although sometimes they may exercise some subtle influence on them. Even if their collective firmness be not negligible, taken individually, the bourgeoisie prove themselves hesitant, insecure, circumspect, and devoid of corporate spirit. So it is that we see the plutocratic elements disintegrate, disavow their own worth, and disperse, subjecting themselves in the second or third generation to the force of attraction of cultural misfortunes, aristocratic assaults, and the old nobility.

On the other hand, a part of the children of the intellectuals, composed of the sons of high state functionaries, moves into industry in search of employment that is more lucrative and provides no less authority and influence than governmental posts. They prefer to satisfy their thirst for empire at the fountain of economic imperialism, which is superior to both pulpit and desk. In German industry, for example, 39 per cent of the salaried directors and other employees come from intellectual environments.[17] Penetration or deviation? Both, but perhaps more the first than the second. Given the uncertainty of the future, and in addition the desire for money and speculation, it is not marvelous if our times particularly are characterized by the intellectual classes suffer-ing grave losses to the professions that the Germans call "practical."

From such a tendency might be born a harmful over-turning and disproportioning of the very social structure of modern nations.[18] The formation of economic elites today is, numerically speaking, outdistancing the formation of intellectual and spiritual elites. Pareto attributes the difficulty of recruit-ment encountered by the Catholic clergy to the growth of more and more new branches of banking and insurance that exert a great attraction on the more promising youths. University professors who like myself have had the fortune to teach in the advanced schools of more than one country, can assert that Pareto's observation holds not only for students of theology, but also for the economists. All too often the best of our disciples, exhorted by us out of the esteem and affection we have for them to aim at a university career, refuse to listen to our advice. Their polite thanks, in fact, have a mocking air about them, for they can scarcely contain their wonder at the remarkable naïveté of professors who are unaware that other and more seductive occupations smile at them. It would take too much time to wait in the anteroom of pure science.

Between the plutocratic elements and the intellectual elements of the political class there is sometimes in force a community of hierarchy equal to that which exists between the economic leaders and the political ones. Such relationships are not fixed but are very elastic. The superior stratum, even if emergent from the masses, can have from time to time a character prevalently intellectual, politico-dynamic, or plutocratic. On the basis of studies of the rise of the intelligentsia in the period of the Renaissance, Simmel believed it could be said that a superior culture is capable of molding a society. He believes that the criterion of intellectuality was sufficient to distinguish the whole social order and to create new classes.[19]

To valorize intelligence in a political sense requires always money and power. If not, the forces of intellect are consumed uselessly in a mere kingdom of dreams or exhaust themselves in acrobatics of erudition or esthetics; in either case, they remain to our view quite sterile.

Political and financial power, in their turn, are not able to depreciate the cultured classes in maintaining their total social contacts. The rare occasions when a non-intellectual or anti-intellectual party, led by self-taught men or depreciators of culture, takes over the reins of government, affirming its adherence to practice alone, show immediately, at the very hour of triumph, the beginning of a new regard for intellectuality. For history shows that culture is an indispensable function of government.[20]

Despite their frequent departures for a career in practical affairs, the intellectuals overcame the plutocracy in two respects. In the first place, by their superior numbers, precisely why they are so poor; and, in the second place, by their greater continuity of biological renewal. In comparison with those of the leading industrial families, the genealogical trees of intellectual families are a good deal older, higher, and consequential, with a full regard for the traditions of generations.

The foundation of the politico-volitive category rests in the lust for authority, in indomitable faith, and in physical courage. That which distinguishes it is its will to power. Its elements can be originally wealthy, and have often made excellent contributions to culture. These are not, however, indispensable traits.

A new political class that forms around a charismatic leader and charismatic group is born outside the traditional hereditary or plutocratic circle. It is endowed with strong abilities and proclaims a transcendental mission, and it is capable of inspiring in its followers a fidelity and a faith that approaches the divine and supernatural. Therefore it holds in contempt in the beginning all contact with economic factors. Says Max Weber, "True charisma is specifically non-economic."[21] Pure charisma is foreign to matters of economy. Pecuniary bonds between the leader and his most faithful followers are not lacking, but they are invested with an honorary character more like charity than like salary.[22]

The intellectuals do not form an economic class. They are to be found at all income levels, so that in the community of culture there is a place for the plutocratic erudite as well as the so-called intellectual proletariat.

And similarly, when we turn to the connection between the intellectuals and the volitive elements of the political class, the intellectuals do not form a political unity, practically by definition. They are accustomed to lead all parties without distinction. Two sub-species, the idealists and the apostates, place themselves by preference at the head of revolutions. The French Revolution was the work of intellectuals. Socialism was inspired and directed throughout by intellectuals, often from the bourgeoisie. It is also known that the nationalist and irredentist movements had a preponderant intellectual stamp to them; they are university movements, professorial movements, student movements. So-called conservative and reactionary states and parties are also in the hands of intellectuals.[23]

In France, students of political science, though approaching the matter from the most divergent points of view ideologically, agree in making the intellectuals the target of their most bitter criticism and in condemning the intermediary function exercised by them in politics. In his book *Le Procès de Socrate* (The Trial of Socrates), 1889, Georges Sorel wrote a disquisition against the inertia and vices of the intellectuals.[24] This antipathy assumed an even more acute form in Sorel's analysis of the Dreyfus trial, which he deemed an "impudent" attempt of the intellectuals to assault authority.

The syndicalist, Edouard Berth, in his book *Les Mefaits des Intellectuels* (The Errors of Intellectuals), described the cultural elements as devoid of any class position,[25] but as acting parasitically and incompetently in the interests of whatsoever economic group. To Charles Maurras, in his work, *L'Avenir de l'Intelligence* (The Future of Intelligence) and to Leon Daudet, intellectuality is the slave of capitalism; it is vacillating and fickle. And it is also the slave of modern democracy that our century has inherited from the "stupid nineteenth century" (Daudet).[26] These two authors maintain that the intellectuals cannot recover their integrity without being depoliticized, while the masses must be deintellectualized because the benefits of intelligence are wasted on them. To achieve this end, an authoritative regime dominated by plutocratic influence is necessary. Charles Péguy writes "of the situation created by the intellectual." Julien Benda stigmatizes the intellectuals whom he calls "the *clercs*" for having betrayed by their necessarily impure contacts with politics their genuine scientific mission, which is more transcendent than material, and requires of them an absolute and undisturbed objectivity.[27] Nor can one deny that, putting the problem on an idealistic plane,[28] the considerations of Benda hit the point.

Several subtle French writers have sought to distinguish between two categories of intellectuals, one organizable, the other non-organizable.[29] Others have uncovered a political antagonism between two different categories, of which each would form the head of one of the two major forces contending for power: the conservative, represented by lawyers (Poincaré, Millerand, "la Droite" composed of rightist politicians), and the radical, represented by university professors, especially from philosophy and affiliated sciences, for the most part coming from the Ecole Normale Supérieure, the "normaliens" (J. Jaurès, Léon Blum, Albert Thomas, Edouard Herriot, "la Gauche"). The prevalence of this last category in contemporary times in France ought to give the country the name "Professors' Republic" (République des Professeurs), according to Thibaudet.[30]

As proclaimed by its doctrines, its practical politics, and the analysis of the occupations of its adherents, fascism is not classist, but comes from varied classes and social categories. Politically speaking, its advent has constituted an irreparable blow to the liberal exponents of middle-class power; fascism has made of strata, groups, and families, politically speaking, a *tabula rasa*. In democratic systems, different political elites are active, all of them led by special "general staffs" and all contending for power. Tenure of power for any one of them is short, while the others wait expectantly to get their chance at ruling. In Fascist regimes, on the contrary, although one may notice some "rotations in office," or, better, changing of the guard, within the ranks of the party itself, its stability and totalitarianism clothe it with a definitively exclusive character, and allow dissenters no hope of return to power. Yet it is permitted to remark, that the vast bureaucratic hierarchy of the party and Fascist state, whether because of its relative youth or its origins, seems fresh. On the economic side, fascism has not yet changed the social composition of the Italian people.[31] However, the rigid application of corporate principles promises to bring numerous and substantial transformations in the future.

Generally speaking, a variety of other changes have taken place. Both politically and economically it has without doubt served as a means of social rise for many elements of the lower middle class. It possesses, among the functionaries of the party an average quality, culturally and socially speaking, lower than that of the liberals of another time. Thus, for example, among 93 federal party secretaries who took office on April 15, 1935, over one-third, 39, were without any advanced scholastic diploma; 25 held doctorates without specification of the field, but among them might be found doctors in business administration or even agriculture; 5 accountants and bookkeepers; 4 engineers, and only 5 professors and 15 lawyers,[32] occupational categories dear to the liberals.

Parliaments have continued to function normally so long as they have been composed of elements taken from the knowledgeable classes, the "notables," that is wherever the deputies were "in a family gathering." They were not yet composed of parties with class orientations, particularly those whose contrasts were based solely on differences in property. With the rise of pure class parties, especially of the proletariat, the position of parliament changed and it is still changing.

But even the bureaucratization of the party as manifested in the American caucus system, conveys the same result, inasmuch as the party acquires a plebiscitary character and causes the delegates to change from being the "masters" of the voters to being the "servants" of the party chiefs. Or so it seemed at least to Max Weber.[33] And our own researches confirm the power of the organization leaders, be they candidates or managers, over the situation, regardless of the voters' desires. Of final and large importance to the decline of parliaments is the replacement of parliamentary bureaucracy by a party bureaucracy, as in Italy. There parliament was reduced to an appendix of the executive power, with brief and widely-spaced sessions. Debate loses its reason for being; professors and lawyers lose their supremacy in consequence, and must become syndical and corporate organizers.

In conclusion, it may be stated that the problems of social and political metabolism are at present deserving of close examination. The World War and its numerous concomitant and succeeding phenomena have produced conspicuous mutations in the composition of the political class, taken either as a whole or in its parts, and these changes are most suggestive in the study of political science, social class, and general economics. It is evident also that the results give confirmation to the theory of the circulation of the elites, that perennial push which gives the state the freshness it needs though sometimes individuals and groups are hurt and often quite badly.

In the years since the war, the law of the circulation of elites has developed, always excepting Russia, not in the sense of the substitution of one class for another, but only in the more restricted and normal sense of the entrance of new elements into the leading class. This process has assumed in the last decade a greatly accelerated rhythm. One finds it in all three sectors of the dominant class—the volitive, the intellectual, and the plutocratic. The influence of the middle classes, and especially the lower middle class rather than the unskilled workers, is rising. The universities, as befits their ancient function, are the switching-grounds where these transferences begin to occur.

Fascism has denied class distinctions on the one hand, but on the other has taken power from the intellectuals and reduced the strength of parliamentarism. Despite their essential differences in most other spheres, Italian Fascism and German National Socialism are equally opposed to academic intellectualism. They have given encouragement to elements peculiarly political—the "volitive type." A less vivid tendency to diminish the role of intellect and economics is also visible in democracies. One can in fact insist that today intellectual and monetary values are subordinated increasingly to other social values. It follows therefrom that serious modifications in the patterns of social metabolism will be produced.

NOTES

1. These are the conclusions of the author on the basis of considerable statistical and general research. See his *Umschichtungen in den herrschenden Klassen nach dem Kriege*, Stuttgart-Berlin: Kohlhammer Verlag, 1934.
2. The average number of children among the higher intellectual families in the United States is 1.87, based on data in *Who's Who in America*, according to Mary Richmond, "The Concern of the Community with Marriage," in Margaret Rich, *Family Life Today*, Boston: Houghton Mifflin, 1928, p. 66.
3. On this theme see, for example, among the more important writers: Abbé de Choisy, *op. cit.*, Otto Konrad Roller, *Die Einwohnerschaft der Stadt Durlach im 18. Jahrhundert in ihren wirtschaftlichen und kulturgeschichtlichen Verhältnissen, dargestellt aus ihren Stammtafeln*, Karlsruhe: Braun, 1907; Werner Sombart, *Der Bourgeois*; René Johannet, *op. cit.* Even German choral societies engaged in rather sharp competition as a result of the diverse social origins of their memberships. The choral society that was the poorest moved into an artistic relationship toward the others that was deemed part of the "class struggle"; see the curious facts related by Hans Staudinger, *Individuum und Gemeinschaft in der Kulturorganisation des Vereins*, Jena: Diederichs, p. 106.
4. Pareto, *I sistemi socialisti*, I, p. 32.
5. Mosca, *Il principio aristocratico e il democratico nel passato e nell' avvenire*, Turin: Paravia, 1903, p. 22.
6. Corrado Gini, *Le basi scientifiche della politica della popolazione*, 1931, p. 245.
7. D'Avenal, *op. cit.*, p. 80.
8. Cf. de Tocqueville, speaking of early nineteenth-century America: "The first thing that strikes one in the United States is the great multitude of those who are seeking to escape from their original social condition; and the second, is the small number of those of lofty ambition that one encounters in the midst of this universal ambition," *op. cit.*, II, p. 132.
9. Hans Kelsen, "Remarks on Democratic Themes," in *Verhandlungen des deutschen Soziologentages*, Sept. 1926, Tübingen: Siebeck, 1927, p. 37.
10. Carlo Pisacane, *Saggio sulla rivoluzione*, 3rd ed., Bologna: Virano, 1894, p. 17. On the socialism of Pisacane, see Nello Rosselli, *Carlo Pisacane nel risorgimento italiano*, Turin: Bocca, 1932, pp. 214, 283–284.
11. P. J. Proudhon, *Les confessions d'un révolutionnaire pour servir à l'histoire de la révolution de février*, new ed., Paris: Librairie Internationale, 1869, pp. 45–54, 65–74.
12. Karl Marx and Friedrich Engels, *The Communist Manifesto*.
13. Cf. Angelo Oliviero Olivetti, *Problemi del socialismo contemporaneo*, Lugano: Scagnoni, 1906, p. 41.
14. *Op. cit.*, I, pp. 458ff, 511 *et passim*.

15. Karl Kautsky, *Klassengegensätze von 1789*, Stoccarda: Dietz, 1889, p. 79.
16. Roberto Michels, *Sunto di storia economica germanica*, Bari: Laterza, 1930, p. 96.
17. J. Nothaas, "Sozialer Auf- und Abstieg im deutschen Volk," in *Beiträge zur Statistik Bayerns*, no. 117, Monaco, Bavaria: Lindauer, 1930, p. 62.
18. For example, E. Martin Saint-Léon is preoccupied with this problem in France. Cf. "La bourgeoisie française et la vie chère," in *Musée Social*, Jan. 1921.
19. Georg Simmel, *Soziologie*, p. 311.
20. This holds true, although in different measure of quantity and quality, for all European, South American, Asiatic, and African states. In America, with certain exceptions in the great universities of the older states, there has been no chance to form that class which in England is called the upper middle class, composed in great part of intellectuals. In the United States, the intellectuals are badly compensated, almost completely devoid of esprit de corps, and they do not maintain a tenor of life that distinguishes them noticeably from other professions or that conforms to the values they represent. They are scarcely different even in moral standards from the bourgeoisie, whose life and ideals they share. (Charlotte Lütkens, *Staat und Gesellschaft in Amerika, Soziologie des amerikanischen Kapitalismus*, Tübingen: Mohr, 1929, p. 157.) As may be seen, cultural environments in which values are not considered except to the extent to which they have practical "use-value" and are accessible to everybody, present indubitable systems of what is termed "colonial" or "pioneer" cultures. This culture has lost recently its basic economic reasons for being, but it still responds morally to special interests.
21. "Wirtschaft und Gesellschaft," *op. cit.*, p. 142.
22. Max Weber, "I tipi del potere," in *Nuova Collana di economisti stranieri ed italiani, Politica ed Economia*, Vol. XII, ed. by Roberto Michels, pp. 227–228.
23. Roberto Michels, *Studi sulla democrazia e sull'autorità*, Florence: Nuova Italia, pp. 79ff, and "Historisch-kritische Untersuchungen zum politischen Verhalten der Intellektuellen," *Schmollers Jahrbuch*, LVII, no. 6 (1933), pp. 29–56.
24. Cf. Michael Freund, *Georges Sorel, der revolutionäre Konservativismus*, Frankfort: V. Klostermann, 1932, pp. 121ff.
25. "Two basic groups of the bourgeoisie are the merchants and the intellectuals," Edouard Berth, *Les méfaits des intellectuels*, Paris: Rivière, 1914, p. 132; cf. p. 137.
26. Berth also adds: "Democracy furnishes nothing but abject servants of an odious, anonymous, and collective tyranny that is presumptuously called a "republic," *loc. cit.*, p. 81.
27. Benda, *La trahison des clercs*, Paris: Grasset, p. 192.
28. See also p. 199.
29. "To each epoch of history corresponds a certain type, the cavalier to the Middle Ages, the honest man to the seventeenth century, the citizen during the Revolution and the nineteenth century. If true that the twentieth century is the century of the producers, the intellectual owns himself to be a producer but also that he is a citizen, an honest man and a cavalier." (Maxime Leroy, cited by José Germain, *Le syndicalisme et l'intelligence: Organisation du travail depuis le guerre*, Paris: Valois

p. 13.) There would be two types of intellectuals, "the technicians of industry (engineers, etc.) who form the disciplined intellectuals" and "the intellectual nobility" (p. 21). Izoulet distinguishes four groups in the French bourgeoisie: the intellectuals with professions, the society intellectuals (useless people, living from rents and women), the Catholics, and the free-thinkers. The first have knowledge but not science; the second have the time to study but timidity and curiosity divert their work; the third have a fine faith, but for that reason are not avid for the results of science; the fourth loves science, but lacks the sacred fire, because, not seeing in nature, in man, and in the state the ideas of eternal struggle, they are basically sceptical (Jean Izoulet, *L'âme française et les universites nouvelles selon l'esprit de la Révolution*, Paris: Colin, 1892, pp. 28–48).

30. Albert Thibaudet, *La république des professeurs*, Paris: Grasset, pp. 201ff.
31. There has been some tendency to improve some land and substitute small farms for the great land holdings with consequent family changes in the direction of greater stability on the land.
32. Figures kindly supplied by Ernesto Lama.
33. Max Weber, "Tipi del potere," *op. cit.*, p. 260.

CHAPTER VI

Charismatic Leadership

RAPID change in social conditions in modern times revived in political science the concept of the elite, which previously seemed to have been totally abandoned. In democratic countries there is no single unit of the political elite. In democracy, indeed, there can be perceived various elites, which in the form of political parties, all governed by a special staff, struggle for power. From this derives that lack of stability, one of the most remarkable characteristics of the system of "rotation in office," as the Americans say, which makes the periods of government of short duration. Now such a system, without doubt, must bring an expenditure of time, a slowing down of necessary training for those who intend to acquire governmental competence. It brings also a great lack of security, of symmetry, and of straightforwardness in the conduct and management of public affairs.

But on the other hand the democratic system offers a certain guarantee to the members of the various elites of the repetition (if not entirely automatic, surely readily foreseeable and not exceedingly difficult of realization) of their turn at the helm of the state. But, be it said parenthetically, these manifold minor elites inevitably become bitter enemies of every government conquered and held by a single strong elite of anti-democratic tendencies. For the latter has an almost permanent character and is based on a principle which prolongs the usual expectation "sine die," actually excluding the majority of the elites from political power. And without the least intention of harming anybody we will say, "Hinc illae lacrimae."

119

In the economic field, the formation of single elites is much harder. It can be affirmed indeed that the scientific search for a theory of the political elite cannot be made with the same criteria that govern a search for an "analogous theory of the elite in economics." For in the political field the mass, having the right or the possibility of abstaining from politics, is effectively and visibly governed by a minority, while in the economic field everybody inevitably must "economize."[1] It happens that, in economics, we are always confronted with a great variety of elites or ruling classes, corresponding to the enormous variety of articles made for profit.

Thus homogeneity is wanting in the businessman type, even when, for defensive or offensive reasons of foreign or internal politics the various types sometimes become allies to the point of forming an apparently compact elite. Such occasional apparent compactness does not prevent there being in the bosom of the elites traces (visible to the naked eye of anybody whose glance is not dimmed by arch-socialist or arch-middle-class prejudices) of strongly different types of economic elites, such as the great professional and patrimonial rentiers,[2] the great industrial and landed interests, the great bankers and the great speculators, the great exporters and the great importers. Neither ought one forget the many struggles of these various elites with one another within the structure of the economically dominant class itself to safeguard their particular economic and social interests and their hegemony in the state.

Inasmuch as the concept of the unified and single elite was born within the sphere, so to speak, of century-old democracy, it inevitably tends to be a critique of the surrounding political society. As such, it employs two essentially dissimilar criteria.

First, the critics of democracy deny the principle of the majority because it seems to them a result of mere accidental appearance. Even if, by chance, the emanations from the activity of the electoral majority can be called rule, this then

could not be anything but a rule by the weak and the un-
knowing, and, therefore, in final analysis, a contradiction in
terms.

The other criterion of those who subject the foundations
of democracy to criticism does not care at all to learn whether
the majority would be capable of governing; it denies that
system from the start. According to them, it is a political
postulate of the greatest value that the right to the management of government never does belong to the majority, but
to the will of the stronger and to the vitality, more indisputable and indomitable, of an individual or of a conscious group
of persons; in sum, of an energic and compact minority.

As Schmitt-Dorotic appropriately observes, in one of his
learned historico-juridical works, dictatorship, more than
being individual, is in the majority of cases, somehow collective.[3] The psychological corollary of such a political trait
would be the existence of a quality which we will call "sincerity." By its nature, the rule of the elite will be frank, clear,
concrete, direct. The elite does not exercise its function by
means of tortuous intrigues and of "connections" dear to
majoritarian and democratic regimes. Nor is it inevitably
prey to lack of clarity, to vacillation, indecision, and to foolish
and insipid compromises. Instead it is secure in the monopolistic control of central power.

This quality has been defined and elaborated by Georges
Sorel, creator of revolutionary syndicalism, who saw in the
worker's syndicate (if only it does not become faint-hearted)
a willing minority, the homogeneous unity of elements, tech-
nically and economically speaking, communalized or com-
munalizable by the similarity of political ideals. The syndi-
cates present, under modern conditions, the required theoretical and dynamic conditions for a lasting tenure in power.
To such an end the organized minority should avail itself
then, says Sorel, of the "myth of the general strike." In addition, prematrimonial sexual purity and the monogamic integrity of the family ought to be steadfast principles of the

elite-to-be.[4] And, on the economic side, the high productive capacities of their own ranks developed from work-discipline in the factories and from the labor unions ought to be used for maximum political action.

The notion of the danger of numbers to the purity of political ideas has been stated by the German Socialists themselves. For example, Weitling complained that the abnegation and devotion of his followers were diminishing directly because of the increase in their ranks.[5] Bebel too was displeased to see how the political successes of the "big party" induced an ever increasing number of egoists, charlatans, and people of doubtful moral character to declare themselves its disciples.[6] And it is strange how Eduard Bernstein, writing a book on the historical development of the Socialist Party, with the interesting title *Von der Sekte zur Partei* (From the Sect to the Party) seems not to grasp the essential side of the question, that is, that the sect, becoming a party, a parliamentarian party besides, inevitably loses its intrinsic cohesion.[7]

Max Weber states that the ruling authority draws its origin from one of the three following forms of legitimacy:[8]

1. "Rational" legitimacy, based on laws and on recognized legal regulations. In the case of rational legitimacy, authority is conferred by general designation of the interested group on a given person. He is supposedly provided with technical and administrative capacities necessary to the chief of a bureaucratic hierarchy, which demands circumscribed and regulated qualifications. Examples would be the elective president of a republic, but also the manager of an industrial concern.

2. "Traditional" legitimacy, based on faith in the sanctity of family rights transmitted from generation to generation. A typical case would be the monarch.

3. "Charismatic" legitimacy, meaning by this a legitimacy based on the spontaneous and voluntary submission of the masses to the rule of persons endowed with extraordinary congenital qualities, sometimes held to be justly supernatural

and in every way always far superior to the general level. By virtue of these qualities such persons are deemed capable (and often they are) of accomplishing great things, and even miraculous things. And for that reason it happens that these men seem ultimately to have been appointed by no less than God Himself. Examples would be the Prophets and the "Duce."

Vincenzo Cuoco (1770–1823) judged the advent of the political "duce" bound to the existence of democracy. He says: "What a very foolish mistake it is, that of trying to find the virtuous man, that is, the rare man, among a very restricted number of men! So it happens that in the oligarchic cities often he is not to be found; whence it is that, in difficult situations, there are often lacking minds and might equal to the needs and the dangers. In the democratic cities, on the contrary, it only rarely occurs that the extraordinary man is not there for the extraordinary needs, because having a greater number to choose from, it is easier to find him."[9] In this sense the precondition for the emergence of leaders consists in democracy or in the free and unconditional process of the "circulation of the elites."

Nonetheless, the possibilities residing in the structure of the elite is only the starting point. The motive and the initially established aims of democracy and charism are very dissimilar. Here we are brought to discuss a basic element in the new theory of the elite. This consists in the institution of the "duce," of whom we will first treat in an abstract and general sense.

Nobody can refrain from observing that the execution of the smallest move requires a quick and able decision. The bad marksman is not always such because his aim is poor or because he does not see the target with sufficient exactness, but sometimes simply because his hand shakes from emotion. Neither is the American philosopher Peirce wrong in affirming that he who fears not being able to reach the other side of the ditch will not succeed in jumping it, not even if he possesses the full physical and technical ability. Whence it is that one of the first requisites of the duce consists in an un-embarrassed, easy deportment, which arises from the faith he has in himself and in his own vocation and mission. When his third parliament asked of Cromwell the justifying docu-ments for his dictatorship, he answered, without fierceness but with profound conviction, by turning the question, saying that he owed his "protectorship" to the same force to which the gentlemen members of the House of Commons owed their so much more modest function, and that, if they denied him his right, they would be forced to deny in consequence their own right. For it was nothing but a reflex and a deriva-tion of his power.[10]

The inherent surety of the legitimacy of one's own social and statal position, however, owes its efficacy also to the collective social trust placed in the chief. Confronted with the charismatic leader, public opinion stands easily bewil-dered, at the mercy of uncontrollable ups and downs. This derives from the fact that public opinion does not take ac-count of the phenomenon that each forward motion is by its nature made up of elements so dissimilar, and accompanied by concomitant phenomena so dissimilar, that in effect progress is not possible in one area without bringing some prejudicial effects in some other. Almost every step in a given direction determines a regression or at least a check in another. Nature itself is subjected to this rule. And progress appears to be subtended to the same restrictive law which rules individu-ality.

From this not even genius is exempted. The man who is endowed with rare qualities, far superior to the average of his fellow creatures, and who represents, so to speak, an incarna-tion of intellectual progress, is thus affected. Not by mistake has genius been called the guide of humanity. The presence of faculties of genius in one empirically, we are almost tempted to add logically, presupposes the coexistence of as many distinct lacunae and deficiencies. Boutroux says, in regard to genius and greatness, that the constitution of man is not sufficient to carry so great a burden. And he adds, following in this respect the footsteps of Pascal, "for a man to do great things and yet be mediocre supposes a rupture of the equilibrium."[11] Lombroso has maintained that genius constitutes a kind of nervous anomaly, a variety of neurosis, a close relative of mental disorder. He has also expressed this view, with some exaggeration, in his duality, "genius and madness." And the best of his German disciples holds as a certainty that "the profound intellect, able to grasp completely and to achieve his objective, is not dissociated from monomania, which is as much to say that a profound intellect is most of the time unilateral."[12]

Not being able to line up without reserve under the Lombrosian flag, it yet appears to us that the evidence of this connection gives valuable support for the analysis of the problem of progress. In the psychology of the man of genius there exist, close to each other—that is, reciprocally conditioning one another—hypertrophically developed sides in the form of eminent faculties and atrophied sides, that is, sides that remain at an inferior level to that of the average man. The weaknesses of great men, which often border upon the ridiculous and are easily observed even by the multitude, even though it does not know the causes, are nothing but the correlative limits of extraordinary qualities, which distinguish leaders by lifting them above their contemporaries. The great writers and poets are for the most part mediocre in those calculations that concern their domestic economy, even when they are good at figures. Great artists, unsurpassed for loftiness of mind, have almost always an infantile naïveté and rare conceptual incapacity. In abstract sciences they cannot find their way out, and most of the time they are not very familiar with the applied art of living. No one better represents the progress of humanity in the highest reaches of sensibility and intuition. However, the progress they personify is one-sided.

The direction of their superiority is inseparable from the regression of their inferiority.

By expecting too much of him, the masses expose the leader and themselves to great danger. The collective social faith in the leader sometimes may assume a distinct mystic form.[13] So it happened that wherever the multitudes thought the "duce" to be almighty, the collective faith collapsed as soon as any natural event belied the supposed omnipotence.[14] The ancient pagan peoples many times expelled an idolized chief if he had been deprived of authority in the eyes of his followers by the eruption of a volcano or by the overflowing of a river with which he had shown himself unable to conjure.[15]

To faith in his own mission is added, in the charismatic leader, born as he is from the masses, the need of remaining in continuous contact with the masses. There derives from this an historico-political phenomenon of greatest importance. It may be said that tempestuous times always find the men, their exponents, who faithfully express them, and that Italy found in its new "Duce" or leader, at least in many ways, "its living and active incarnation." And it appears to be true that when Mussolini speaks, he translates in a naked and brilliant form the aims of the multitude. The multitude itself frantically acclaims, answering from the profundity of its own moral beliefs, or, even more profound, of its own subconscious.

However, to preserve intact his ascendancy over the mass it is necessary that the charismatic leader remain distinct from it and not share his faults with it. Above all it is important that he should not share certain sympathies and natural aversions, and some human weaknesses. To express ourselves better, allow us to refer to another kind of rule, apparently quite dissimilar, but, for those who can perceive it, intimately related with what we are now expounding. Let us go into the matter of the feminine mind. The coquette who acquires some value in the eyes of men is one who although stimulating their concupiscence, remains essentially cold and impassive; the coquette does not give herself up; rather, maintaining the fiction that she may let herself be won over by the other's desire, she maintains a demeanor which makes it doubtful whether she is even made of flesh and bones. But the coquette, by her apparent or genuine frigidity, acquires a great superiority over other women who do not conceal their impulses. So it happens that the coquette is ordinarily much more courted, and to overcome her resistance the lover is often forced to give her the greatest satisfaction that man can give to woman, that of marrying her, the lover considering matrimony indissoluble and the only means to keep her in his possession. As the coquette acts, so also does the leader of the democratic party. Keeping the distance which separates him from the common people he also will finally make himself precious and indispensable.

The ascetic, renouncing all the enjoyments of life and withdrawing from the mass, also prepares for himself the pedestal of his sanctification. For the fact that the ascetic leads an abnormal life, based as it is on abstention from goods and values that they cannot disregard and believe to be congenital, makes most men think they perceive in him a supernatural being. Also the influence exerted by the prophet increases and decreases in direct relation to this success or failure in rejecting his instincts and immaterializing himself.

Now, all things being equal, it is obligatory that even the missionary or the politician be subjected to the same psychological laws and use them with the aim of doing good. Not to bear the deleterious influx of the collective psychology and not to let himself be absorbed by the mass, it is necessary that the leader interrupt, at short intervals, the continuity of his contact with them. So as not to form a part of it, it is convenient that once in a while he break away from it. Of this sociological necessity scholarly Americans, French, and Germans have brought forward several historical and psychological examples. We will add another: the Jesuits, who, to avoid forming a part of the mass, that is, to maintain intact their superiority and their rule over the masses, for centuries have employed a system by which they alternate periods of life lived among the crowds with periods of complete isolation, for the psychology of the mass is always made up of mediocrity and impenetrable grayness. However, the leader of a political elite adopting the above-mentioned method will not act by calculation or indifference as the coquette, nor by mystical sanctity and human reservedness as the prophet, but out of a healthy rule of life and essentially out of passion for the mass itself, whose welfare seems inseparably united to his own potential and affective existence.

However, the powerful man laden with responsibility does not waste his time. It is a historical truth that the great dynasts have led a very active, laborious life. Louis XIV of France was accustomed to convoke his council of state on the average of at least three times a week.[16] Frederick the Great considered himself the first servant of the state[17] and notwithstanding his various philosophical, poetical, and musical dispositions, he behaved as such. Napoleon I used to take active and factitive interest in everything that concerned his vast empire, from the military art to the Chamber of Commerce and fashions. There is also the example of another powerful man, Mussolini, addicted perhaps even excessively to work.[18]

The man who was not born as a leader of the masses but made himself such, is he good? This question has often been posed, sometimes even ingenuously. Mosca answers: "It should be known at once that 'goodness' in this sense, which is after all the literal one, is a quality which refers very much to others and almost always very slightly to those who use and presumably possess it. It at most becomes a little obnoxious when it is found in persons born or arrived, almost casually, at a social position so exalted as to take away every temptation from those who might want to abuse it. . . ."[19]

And he continues: "To go up the social staircase, even in calm and normal times, the first requisite is without doubt the constant capacity for work, but, immediately after comes the ambition, the unswerving will to go ahead, to excel over one's fellow men, and this ill befits an excessive sensibility and, let us even say it, goodness. For such 'goodness' cannot remain indifferent to the sufferings of those who, if he is to go ahead, must be pushed back, and, when truly profound and felt, it hesitates to calculate the merits, the rights, and the sorrows of the others less than its own. And it may seem strange at first sight that men, who generally would like to see that their rulers had the most exquisite and loftiest moral qualities and that they should think much about public welfare and little about their own, then, when it concerns themselves, and above all when they try to go ahead and to arrive, if they can, at the most eminent positions, they generally do not care to observe those precepts which they would like to see as a constant guide for their superiors. All that could justly be required of leaders is not to become inferior to the average moral level of the society they rule, to identify to a certain extent their welfare with that of the public, and not to commit any too vile, mean, and repugnant actions of a kind to disqualify, in the ambit in which he lives, the man who has committed them."[20]

And that is right. Goodness, for those that are at the helm of a nation, does not signify sentimentality, but sentimental concentration on public welfare, abnegation, complete and unconditional devotion. The great monarchs have not been without this essential requisite of the people's ruler. They have been of an energetic goodness, of a goodness not separated from fierceness.[21] The popular leader who does not act out of mere personal ambition, but because guided by a high ideality, and knows (as arduous to know as anything) how to escape the constant temptation of megalomania, mortal enemy of good sense and of "objective" affection for the country, surely may be even better.

The charismatic government makes only sparing use of the bureaucracy. The leader does not operate always through career functionaries, but chooses his collaborators according to their charismatic qualifications, and on the basis of his inspiration. They are persons who up to the time under discussion have remained out of the ruling and bureaucratic classes. Consequently their rank does not imply lasting character but will always be taken from them, as soon as their supposed charismatic qualification fades out.

Since this is the case, it is useless, anti-historical, and anti-scientific to hope that dictatorships, having happily initiated their political work, will abdicate at the height of their power, since abdication is an act of weakness. It implies that the dictator will feel that he has nothing more to say and nothing else to do; or it implies that such an act might be voluntary on the part of him who, finding himself pressed continually by misfortune or bold and confident adversaries, judges it impossible to continue on the given path, and supinely prefers an inglorious disappearance to a glorious fall. The charismatic leader does not abdicate, not even when water reaches to his throat. Precisely in his readiness to die lies one element of his force and triumph. He will abdicate only when he is seized from within by extreme bitterness and repugnance; in such a case it means he has lost his charisma. For the charismatic leader does not beseech the multitude; rather, when occasion arises, he will know how to chastise it, and he takes for granted, in his mission, the adaptability of the masses to his plans.

But, if the charismatic duce, so long as he so remains, shuns political suicide, and is intransigent and radical, this does not signify that his radicalism and his intransigence is absolute and deprived of political wisdom and of obvious wariness. In England, John Morley conceives compromise essentially under two forms: in the form willingly slow and prudent, given to the affirmation of one's own ideas, with the intent of gradually making them enter others' attitudes, and, secondly, in distinct aptitudes for elementary defense, which in their turn lead to two dissimilar practical behavior-patterns: tacit submission because of cowardliness and dignified silence after having enunciated one's own dissent.

However, withal Morley simply characterizes some empirical methods of bargaining with the realities of force. He does not characterize at all the essence and the laws of theoretical compromise, thus overlooking certain developments that are to be found in the history of political theories.[22] Looking at it this way, it can be said that all politics consist in an uninterrupted series of compromises, and we will define compromise in this sense in two manners. Compromise is the partial renunciation of political theories which have been shown as impracticable and inapplicable in time and in space, be it for their inherent impracticability and inapplicability or be it only because they contrast with concrete tendencies which will remain irremovable for a long period of time. There is also a compromise which we will call passive and which consists in incorporating, often imperceptibly, extraneous concepts, heterogeneous by their nature, into our political system. In this last case, compromise is to be compared to the teeth of time, that gnaw at everything and that, taken "sub specie aeternitatis," leave no political idea unaltered, no matter how pure and unalterable it may appear.

Presupposed and placed in relation to the above-mentioned limits, the charismatic government is averse to some compromises which its messianic logic holds to be vile and contemptible. Rather, its perfect faith in itself, essential basis of this form of charismatic government, furnishes an inherent dynamic tendency. And that for two reasons. The charismatic leader has a past of struggles—victorious struggles. Therefore he is conscious of his qualities which he has demonstrated capable of valuable use. It so happens that the charismatic leader likes to live a dangerous life, such as has been indicated by Friedrich Nietzsche and which Benito Mussolini has many times eulogized with glowing words. On the other side his future is bound to the proofs that he may furnish of the faithfulness of his star.

And then, the political leader, unless his dynamic stimulus is made of vulgar personal ambition, inevitably cherishes a

super-personal and often righteous super-terrestial idea. Therefore, and from his necessity for struggle, and his intensity of
hope, he will be an evangelist, whose passion aims at the
attainment of remote and lofty goals. That such is the case
did not remain hidden to practical French philosophy of the
seventeenth century. Says La Rochefoucauld: "The great
spirits are not those who have less of passion and more of virtues than common souls, but those who simply have the greatest plans."[23] On his deathbed the great Saint-Simon voiced a
phrase that expresses at the same time a warning and an
advice. "Remember," he said to one of his disciples, "that
to do great things requires great passions."[24] Such passion
cannot but arise from that quality that theoretical sociology
has wanted to call the expression of the naked ego itself, the
basis of every power of suggestion on the masses.[25]

NOTES

1. Carlo Emilio Ferri, *Lineamenti di una teorica delle elites in economia.*
   Milano: Istituto Editoriale Scientifico, 1925, p. 10.
2. Achille Loria, *La sintesi economica.* Torino: Bocca, 1909.
3. Carl Schmitt-Dorotic, *Die Diktatur.* München: Duncker, 1921, p. v.
4. Agostino Lanzillo, *Giorgio Sorel, con una lettera autobiografica.* Roma:
   Libr. Ed. Romana, 1910.
5. Charlotte von Reichenau, "Wilhelm Weitling," in *Schmollers Jahrbuch
   für Gesetzgebung,* 49 Jahrg., 2. Heft, 1925, p. 326.
6. August Bebel, "Ein Nachwort zur Vizepräsidentenfrage und Verwand-
   tem," in *Neue Zeit,* 1903.
7. Eduard Bernstein, *Von der Sekte zur Partei.* Jena: Diederichs, 1911.
8. Max Weber, "Wirtschaft und Gesellschaft," *Grundriss der Socialö-
   konomik,* Pt. III, Tübingen: Siebeck, 1925, Vol. I, pp. 140ff.
9. Domenico Bulferetti, *Vincenzo Cuoco (1770–1823) Storia, Politica,
   Pedagogia.* Torino: Paravia, p. 50.
10. Thomas Carlyle, *On Heroes, Hero-worship and the Heroic in History.*
    Leipzig: Tauchnitz, 1916, p. 278.
11. Boutroux, in *Foi et vie,* Jan. 16, 1913, p. 35.
12. Hans Kurella, *Die Intellektuellen und die Gesellschaft. Beitrag zur
    Naturgeschichte begabter Familien.* Wiesbaden: Bergmann, 1912, p. 16.
13. "When one speaks of Bonaparte they (the soldiers of the French army in
    Italy) listen with pleasure as if I were speaking of their mistress."
    (V. De Bonstetten, *L'Homme du Midi et l'Homme du Nord ou In-
    fluence du Climat,* Genève: Paschoud, 1824, p. 209.)
14. "Give a child exaggerated notions of his parents' power, and it will
    by-and-by cry for the moon. Let a people believe in government-
    omnipotence, and they will be pretty certain to get up revolutions to

achieve impossibilities." (Herbert Spencer, *Social Statics, or the Conditions Essential to Human Happiness Specified and the First of them Developed.* London: Williams, 1868, p. 319.)

15. Max Weber, "Wirtschaft und Gesellschaft," *op. cit.*, p. 140.
16. "Three times a week, or more often, depending on the urgency of the case, Louis XIV held council. The minister charged with a matter gave his report, which was discussed by his colleagues. Then the sovereign decision of the king closed the debate." G. Lacour-Gayet, "Louis XIV, la Monarchie, absolue Gouverment, Administration, Société," in Ernest Lavisse et Alfred Rambaud, *Louis XIV*, Paris: Colin, 1895, p. 162.
17. Cf. the famous words of the king about "the Prince being the first servant of his state." *Memoires pour servir à l'Histoire de Brandebourg, de Main de Maître* (Frederick II himself), *Imprimie pour la Satisfaction du Public.* Berlin, 1758, Vol. III, p. 30.
18. Suffice as a proof a very recent example. In one of his speeches, on March 7, 1923, at the Ministry of Finance on occasion of the consignment of the budgets to the Presidency, Benito Mussolini said, addressing himself to the functionaries of the Ministry present at the ceremony: "I am happy to be before you because the Minister has spoken well of the high officials of the Ministry of Finance. He has told me that some of you work often as much as 16 hours a day. It is too many hours, and it is a magnificent example. But if such hours were not sufficient, we ought to work even 20 hours." Benito Mussolini, *La nuova politica dell' Italia. Discorsi e dichiarazioni.* Ed. by Amedeo Giannini, Milano: Imperia, 1923, p. 82.
19. Mosca, *Elementi*, p. 458.
20. *Ibid.*, pp. 458–459.
21. Mirabeau, *L'ami des Hommes ou Traité de la Population.* Vol. II, p. 10: "Louis XIV was good, even if fierce."
22. John Morley, *On Compromise*, 2nd ed. London: Chapman, 1877, pp. 84 and 168.
23. Cf. also Henry Joly, *Psychologie des Grand Hommes*, 4th ed. Paris: Spes. 1925, pp. 24ff.
24. Maxime Leroy, *Saint-Simon.* Paris: Rivière, 1925.
25. Alfred Vierkandt, *Gesellschaftslehre.* Stuttgart: Enke, 1923, p. 217.

CHAPTER VII

The Sociological Character of Political Parties

THE political party, etymologically and logically, can embrace only a part of the citizenry, politically organized. The party is a fraction; it is *pars pro toto*. Let us endeavor briefly to analyze its causal origin and its behavior.

According to Max Weber, the political party has a dual teleology. It is a spontaneous society of propaganda and of agitation seeking to acquire power, in order to procure thereby for its active militant adherents chances, ideal and material, for the realization either of objective aims or of personal advantages, or of both. Consequently, the general orientation of the political party, whether in its personal or impersonal aspect, is that of *Machtstreben* (striving to power).[1]

KINDS OF POLITICAL PARTIES

In the personal aspect, parties are often based on the protection accorded inferiors by a strong man. In the Prussian diet of 1855, which was composed of a large number of political groups, each was given the name of its leader. There were the groups of Count de Schlieffen, of Count Arnim, of Tietz, of Karl, of von Patow, of von Vincke, of von Bethmann-Hollweg, of Reichensperger and Mallinkrodt (the last being Catholic). The only group which was called by its true name was a national one, the Polish party.[2]

The history of the labor movement shows that the socialists have not abandoned this "bourgeois" tradition. The socialist parties, on the contrary, have often so completely identified themselves with a leader that they have more or less officially assumed his name, as though to proclaim that they were his property. In Germany, between 1863 and 1875, the rival social-ist factions, courting the favor of the mass of workingmen, were the Marxists and the Lassallians. In France, more re-cently, the great current of socialism was divided into the Broussists, the Allemanists, the Blanquists, the Guesdists, and the Jaurèsists. It is true that the men who so gave their names to different separatist movements personified as com-pletely as possible the ideas and the disposition with which the party was inspired, and which guided them throughout the whole course of their evolution;[3] but it must be admitted, on the other hand, that when the party assumes the name of its leader it is carrying the regard of the herd for its shepherd a bit too far.

Perhaps there is here an analogy between political party and religious sects or monastic orders. Yves-Guyot justly re-marked that the individual belonging to a modern party acts after the same fashion as did the mediaeval monks, who, faithful as they were to the precepts of their masters, called themselves after St. Dominicus, St. Benedictus, St. Au-gustinius, and St. Franciscus, respectively, the Dominicans, the Benedictines, the Augustines, and the Franciscans.[4] These are the types of party which one may designate as the parties of patronage. If the leader exercises his influence over his fol-lowers by qualities so striking that they seem to them super-natural, one can call him a charismatic chief.

This sort of party, the charismatic, takes on varying forms. Ferdinand Lassalle himself, the leader of the Lassallians, was officially merely president of the Allgemeiner Deutscher Arbeiterverein. But he was its president for life. All the main characteristics of leadership were united in him: force of will, wide knowledge, ambition and self-sufficiency, reputation for disinterestedness, celebrity, persuasive oratorship. It pleased him to encourage his followers in idolatry of which he was made the object by the delirious masses and the white-clad virgins who chanted praises to him and offered him bouquets. But not only was, in the case of Lassalle, the charismatic faith the ripe fruit of a psychology which was exuberant and megalomaniacal, but it also was in agreement with the theoretical conception of the hero. We must, he said to the workingmen of the Rhine, in offering them his ideas on the organization of the political party, out of all our scattered desires forge a hammer and place it in the hands of a man whose intelligence, character, and devotion would be to us a guaranty that with the hammer he will strike hard.[5] That is the hammer of the dictator, as he was in fact.

In later periods of history, when the masses demanded at least a simulacrum of democracy and group control in party affairs, and when especially the burning jealousy among the ever-increasing number of leaders admitted no longer, in the socialist movement, the dictatorship of one man, the striking individualities among the leaders, such as August Bebel and Jean Jaurès, were obliged to restrain, as much as possible, these desires and jealousies. Surely, Bebel and Jaurès were two quite different types of charismatic leaders. The one was an orphan of a Pomeranian sergeant, the other a university professor of southern France. The former possessed hauteur and was as imperious as his cousin, the Kaiser (whence the nickname "Kaiser Bebel" which Gustave Hervé attempted to fix upon him); the latter was an orator without peer, fiery, romantic as well as realistic, seeking to surmount difficulties by seriating problems and to resolve them as fast as they presented themselves.[6] Yet the two great leaders, at once friends and enemies, had in common an indomitable faith both in the efficacy of their action and in the historical destiny of the cohorts whose standard-bearers they were. So both became deified—the Prussian, still during his lifetime; the Frenchman, only, alas, after his death.

Moreover, the present offers to discreet sociologists another example of a great leader of a party which regards him as apostle and seer. In Italy, Benito Mussolini differs from the other men whom we have just mentioned in this: he is not only the leader of a great party, he has become also the leader of a great state. With him the axiom, "The party, it is I," has assumed, not only with regard to powerfulness and consciousness, but also with regard to responsibility and assiduous labor, its maximum development. It is very interesting to see how far the masses understand and develop Mussolini's ideals even beyond his own concept. When, after having barely escaped (only some hours before) an attempt on his life, Mussolini, from the balcony of the Palazzo Chigi, harangued an agitated crowd of ten thousand people, explaining to them Italy's situation and the dangers she would have encountered if he had been killed, a voice was raised from the edge of the throng—immediately to be drowned by thunderous applause: "*Tu sei l'Italia*" ("But you are Italy itself"). With these words the interrupter meant to say (and the applauding crowd accentuated the sentiment) that there is really no difference between Mussolini the man and Italy the country, and that the death of the one would undoubtedly be followed by the complete ruin of the other. The leader of the Fascist party himself openly manifested the charismatic quintessence of his character when, after another attempt on his life, he sent a telegram to his Fascist comrades at Bologna urging them to be certain, absolutely certain, that nothing serious could happen to him before he had completed his task.

We do not here have to indicate the dangers such an idea involves in politics. We shall, however, make one strictly sociological observation. It is evident that charismatic leadership like this bears within itself political dynamics of the utmost vigor. The great Saint-Simon on his deathbed told his disciples, it must be remembered, that in order to do great things one must be impassioned. But to be zealous means to have the gift of inciting the zeal of others. It is, in effect, a formidable goad. This is the advantage of charismatic parties over parties with a well-defined program and a class interest. It is true, on the other hand, that the duration of the former is often circumscribed by the duration of their verve and enthusiasm, which sometimes furnish only a very fragile basis. So we see the charismatic parties induced to rest their appeal, in addition to enthusiasm, as much as possible on institutions more durable than human emotions, such, for example, as protective, workers', and professional organizations and interests.

Charism thus lends itself to all political views, no matter of what complexion. All political parties can be provided with charismatic chiefs. Particularly is this true of young, ardent, doctrinaire parties, although, to be sure, charismatic chiefs are sometimes found in parties of more flexible beliefs. In general, charismatic leaders are, as regards political parties, primary phenomena. In other words, they are the founders of them; it is they who engender and start parties. But the history of political parties demonstrates also that there is a certain number of inverse cases. Then it is the party which is the primary phenomenon. From the chronological point of view the leaders are then secondary; that is to say, they appear later, when the party is already active. But that in no way diminishes the intensity of their force, once acknowledged, provided that the pre-existing party is without other leaders of equal value.

In the second place, there are parties which have for their bases, a priori, interests of economic and social classes.[7] And these are especially workers' parties or parties of peasants or of the lower middle class—what the French call "les petites gens"—since the bourgeoisie cannot, by itself, form a party. It is necessary to add still a third category composed of political parties which have been inspired by political or moral ideas —general and abstract—of a *Weltanschauung*. When this conception rests on a more developed and minutely elaborated dogma, one can speak of doctrinaire parties whose doctrines are, however, a privilege of leaders. Here we are in the presence of parties of free trade or protection, or of those which speak of the rights of liberty or of justice (To each the fruit of his labor; or, To each according to his abilities; or, To each according to his needs), or, again, of those which speak of authority.

It is, however, evident that this differentiation into parties of patronage, parties of social or economic interest, and parties of doctrinaire consistency is neither sharp nor final. It is not sharp, for the simple reason that past and present parties represent, in large degree, intermediate nuances or combinations, in which the competent observer will not fail immediately to recognize the existence, sometimes in very unequal proportions, of constituent elements of all three categories. At all events, there is no doubt that the program (which is, so to speak, the codification of political beliefs that have given birth to organization) can, in the first category—based as it is entirely on the faith and authority of a singe person—be rudimentary; while it is undeniable that the two other categories, and the second, perhaps, still more than the third, require well developed programs. But even for the doctrinaire parties it may be true to say, with P. Orman Ray, that the principles of a party are apt to be most conspicuous in its early or formative period, while in its later history politics are likely to overshadow principles.[8]

It seems to us, however, that there are still two categories of political parties which, while approaching in a certain sense parties based on principles, have nevertheless characteristics belonging to other types of party that distinguish them somewhat from their analogues. These are the confessional parties and the national parties. The former profess to have, not merely a *Weltanschauung* (theory of life) but an *Ueberweltanschauung* (theory of metaphysical life, a belief). They are the parties seeking to adapt the needs of life here below, envisaged as a preparatory phase, to the immortal life of the soul. The latter, the nationalist parties, may assuredly have ideas both general and universal; they may, for example, proclaim, with the Italian Irredentists, with Stanislao Mancini and Terenzio Mamiani, the principle of nationality, understood in its true sense as the right of each people, and of each fraction of a people, to complete, unconditioned sovereignty.[9] However, at least ever since 1870, the national parties practicing this ideal have transformed themselves into nationalistic parties. These are, in a sense, more limited and devoid of general principles, because one cannot conceive of a general principle which stops at the frontier, or, still worse, which crosses it only to refuse to other nationalities the claims to liberty and freedom which they jealously reserve for themselves.

It is, nevertheless, equally true that many other political principles in the course of time function in a manner exactly opposite to their original and general aims, e.g., the principle of freedom of thought. One can say that optimists are, in general, extremist theoreticians. The consequences of this have been well put by Georges Sorel in writing of the Jacobins: "If, unfortunately, they find themselves armed with great political power allowing them to realize an ideal that they have conceived, optimists may lead their country to worse catastrophes. They are not long in recognizing, indeed, that social transformations are not achieved with the facility they had expected; they attribute their disappointments to their contemporaries, rather than explain the march of events in terms of historic necessity; thus they end by attempting to remove those people whose evil desires seem to them dangerous to the welfare of mankind. During the Terror, the men who spilt most blood were exactly those who had the keenest desire to enable their fellow-creatures to enjoy the golden age of which they had dreamed, and who had the strongest sympathy for human misery. Optimistic, idealistic, and sensitive, as they were, these men showed themselves the more inexorable as they had a greater thirst for universal well-being."[10]

But if the unconscious identification of finalities—material or immaterial, it matters little—with the general good seems to be an absolute law of our spirit, it is none the less true that of all the social groups it is the national political party which uses and abuses this principle the most. For each nation believes that it must accomplish missions, either of liberty (the French in the Revolution), or of order (the Germans under William II), or of civilization (the "white man's burden"), or of discipline, or of morality, or of other ideals. All of these concur in endowing them with presumptive rights over neighboring peoples, who are judged incapable of facing their jobs without being forced to obey orders issued by the missionary people. The good faith, which very often springs from this idea of a mission, communicating itself to national collectivities, gives them the aplomb and energy of which they have need in order to achieve their goals. This is as much as to say that those critics who estimate that in their aggressive actions national groups are fundamentally ferocious and savage are profoundly wrong. At bottom, this ferocity and savagery which cause people to trample under foot and wipe out the interests and aspirations of others are only the forms in which the missionary—and almost always the visionary—conviction manifests itself. Missionary peoples are ferocious and savage not in their feelings but in their actions.

However, as I have attempted to prove in one of my books,[11] the need for organization (what Americans call machinery) and the ineluctable tendencies of human psychology, individual and group, cause distinctions of origin in the main to disappear. The political party as such has its own peculiar soul, independent of the programs and rules which it possesses and the eternal principles with which it is embued. The psychology of the crowd is fairly the same in the socialists and the nationalists, in the liberals and the conservatives. In group movements, with rare exceptions everything proceeds naturally, and not "artificially." The fact that the people follow their leader is quite a natural phenomenon. "To use the term exactly," Rousseau has said, "there has never existed a true democracy, and none can ever exist. It is against natural order that the great number should govern and that the few should be governed."[12] Our consistent knowledge of the political life of the principal civilized nations of the world authorizes us to assert that the tendency toward oligarchy constitutes one of the historic necessities, one of the iron laws of history, from which the most democratic modern societies and, within those societies, the most advanced parties, have been unable to escape.[18]

By giving themselves leaders, the workers create with their own hands new masters, whose principal means of domination consists in their technical and intellectual superiority and in the inability of the masses to control the execution of their commands to the leaders. In this respect, the intellectual has played a role in party politics which has many times been the subject of profound study. Moreover, the mechanism of the socialist party offers to the workers, thanks to the numerous salaried and honorary positions of which it disposes, a possibility of making a career, which exercises on them a force of considerable attraction. Now, to the degree that the political calling becomes complicated and the rules of social legislation multiplied, there is imposed on the leaders of political parties an existence more and more professionalized, based on a continuously widening knowledge, savoir-faire, routine, and sometimes delicate finesse. This is why the distance between the leaders and the led grows constantly greater. Thus one can place one's finger upon the flagrant contradiction which exists, in mature parties, between democratic declarations and intentions, on the one hand, and the concrete oligarchic reality, on the other. Hence the continuous raising of conflicts, often Shakespearian in character, in which the comic borders upon the tragic. It may, therefore, be said that the organization constitutes precisely the source whence conservative currents debouch upon the plain of democracy, causing devastating inundations which render that plain unrecognizable.

Such a *Götterdämmerung* can in no way surprise analytic and alert spirits. Long ago Adam Smith's teacher, the Scottish philosopher Hutcheson, remarked that the patience of the people has always been too great and its veneration for its leaders too inept.[14] Furthermore, for Pareto, the contemporary era is in no way characterized by the augmentation of sociality and the diminution of individualism. Fundamentally, it can be only a question of a quadrille chassé-croisé. For example, the sentiment of subordination, which was manifested in former days by the subjection, more or less voluntary, of inferior classes to superior classes, has today merely been replaced by the submission of the inferior classes to the leader of their party, the syndicate and the strike, and by the submission, less apparent, of the superior classes to the scum of the people, who have never been the object of so much flattery as in the present.[15] And Gabriel Tarde has referred to two correlative sentiments of modern times, namely, the morbid mistrust of the democratic public for its master, and the fear, the malice, the insipidity of the so-called master who submits to all the orders of his inferiors.[16] Naturally, experience informs us that the sycophant and demagogic chief himself considers flattery merely as a means, his aim being always that of dominating the crowd. The democracy clings to the lofty rungs of the orator's ladder, Charles Maurras has said, just like a woman—for the mob is feminine—whose imagination greets with transport the element which is able to excite her.[17] And Thomas Carlyle well stated before him: "No British man can attain to be a statesman or chief of workers till he has first proved himself a chief of talkers."[18]

THE DEMOCRATIC APPEALS

Democracy is of a massive nature. Therefore it cannot function without masses. Parliamentarism presupposes electionism, electionism implies electoral masses.[19] It follows from this that political parties are in vain partly aristocratic in origin and in aim; for it is none the less true that they are forced to make use of the masses. At election time, the *aristoi* candidates deign to descend from their mansions and to bestir themselves among the yokels in order to obtain the majority

in their districts.[20] That is not astonishing. They are not indeed
ridiculous enough to speak in these solemn and decisive
moments for the privilege of minorities, and to restrict themselves to accepting exclusively the votes of that portion of
their fellow men who are sole possessors of the governing
vocation. Inasmuch as they must rely upon the medium of
election, the aristocratic parties make the best of a bad job.
After all, the aristocrats cling to the hope of persuading the
masses indirectly to renounce their own rights by their own
votes. It is, at bottom, the ideal of the Prussian Junkers and
the French aristocrats, who, to democratize themselves, dis-
card the cast-off garments of royalty. Moreover, parties of
huge economic and social classes or interests also follow this
method of camouflage very closely. The majority parties also
take care, in political elections, to address themselves not
alone to their associates. In democracy every one appeals to
the people, to every one of the people, without discrimination.
The Socialist party—the most strictly proletarian—does not
hesitate to solicit openly, at the proper time, the suffrage of
artisans, peasants, and petty bourgeoisie. A Socialist who
before the elections, and afterward, has only a very narrow
conception of what is meant by the working class, loves, during the campaign, to stretch the theoretical extent of this
class to the point of including capitalists, providing, of course,
that they are not too refractory to accord to their employees,
in such a case, some small wage increment.

	This tendency, immanent in contemporary political life,
and which a wag would be tempted to denominate a game
of hide-and-seek, manifests itself even in the names that political parties are accustomed to give themselves in democratic
countries. Indeed, in a democracy, political parties tend to
envelop themselves in a very thick terminological fog, and one
of nearly even color. Here are a few modern political nomen-
clatures. In France, the Liberal Action, the Progressive Republicans, the Republican Union, the Democratic Left, the
Radical Left, the Radical-Socialist Republicans, the Socialist

Republicans.[21] In Germany, the German Popular party, the German People's National party, the German People's party, the Democratic party, the Social Democratic party, and the Christian People's party. In Switzerland the names of political parties differ scarcely at all from those used among their larger neighbors. One would say that no party is distinguishable from the others. All the German and French parties are more or less equally "popular," "democratic," and "national." This tendency is a beautiful example, indeed, of the application of Darwin's law of adaptation to environment carried over into the political field. It is almost cryptic mimicry. In the French elections of 1848 the candidates of almost all shades of political opinion liked to call themselves workers and socialists, in homage to the first universal suffrage.[22] Nowadays they are all democratic.

The influence which the omnibus tendency exerts on political parties is also very distinctly apparent in the tactics of the confessional parties. Let us remember, for example, that in the most important countries of Europe, where there is a Catholic party it has the habit of carefully concealing its essential character by the designations it uses. None ventures to call itself Catholic. In Italy, the Catholic party calls itself, quite simply, "Popular"; in Germany, it becomes the "Center party." But further: the latter party offers strong inducements to have among its members, even among its official representatives, a certain number of Protestants.[23] In Italy, at the congress held by the Catholic party at Easter, 1923, in Turin, Don Sturzo, under the pretext that a party truly Catholic is a *contradictio in adjecto* (the word Catholic signifying universal, and the word party signifying partial), advanced the thesis that his party should be strongly non-confessional.[24] This omnibus tendency has penetrated even into parliament. If this needs demonstration, it will suffice to cite, in France, the paradoxical existence in the Palais Bourbon, in addition to the politically constituted groups, of a "group of deputies not enrolled in any group," which includes men of every shade of opinion, and which even names a bureau.[25]

There is, of course, among political parties a differentiating tendency, which we shall designate a centrifugal tendency, by which they are induced to distinguish themselves one from another, whether in their program and theoretical basis or in their daily manifestations. Moreover, this tendency seems to be repressed and often diverted by a much stronger tendency inherent in all political parties. This is the integrative tendency of the numerical maximum, mortal enemy to all freedom of program and of thought. It is a centripetal tendency, and, in fact, only the logical consequence of the fundamental tendency that dominates the life of political parties, namely, the tendency toward the conquest of the state. Where there are only two parties, as in America, this system is already the extreme expression of the victory of the centripetal tendency over the centrifugal. This victory seems still more manifest considering the fact that the Democrats and the Republicans are at present almost devoid of theoretical or programmatical differences, so that they can both address themselves to the electorate without any "ballast" of differentiating ideas.

FALSE PARTY CLASSIFICATIONS

In truth, the *raison d'être* of the political party is the push for power. Here the objectives certainly differ, some wishing to reach their goal in a peaceful fashion, without agitation (evolutionary as it were). Others, believing that by evolutionary methods they may never attain their ends, prefer an action or a series of actions more vigorous and rapid, by tactics called revolutionary. And it is likewise obvious that the conceptions of political parties are no more identical in the action to be taken after success—action which will depend, at least in principle, on conceptions which they have formed of the role of the state, and which may, in theory, even contemplate its abolition. For to destroy, it is necessary first to capture. At any rate, the first stage of the political party is determined by its ardent desire to absorb power, to become the state. Also the final goal of the party consists in statization. This is why, while awaiting utopia, the party will try to establish at the outset as much as possible a little state within the state. One may thus sustain the thesis that the most accomplished political party will be that one which will have created in its own ranks all the organizing and intellectual details of a nature to make it capable some day to assume the functions of the state, in complete form, just as Minerva issued fully armed from the brain of Jupiter.

It will be worth while to deal briefly with Vilfredo Pareto's theory of political parties. Like Max Weber, the author of these lines, and others, Pareto begins with the premise that political parties seek power. He then divides parties into two essential groups. First, there are the parties which devote themselves to government. This group embraces alike the party in power and those that do not hold it but aspire to it with good chance, and that meanwhile form the parties of opposition. Second, there are the intransigent parties which would hardly attain power. These last contain a greater number of fanatics, but also of honest men, than the other parties which are less ferocious but likewise more depraved.[26] Let us note in passing that, according to an axiom of Italian juridical sociology, it is not a universal supposition that a government is composed of honest men. An eminent Italian sociologist, Gaetano Mosca, considers it even difficult for an honest man, having achieved the realization of his political ambitions, to resist deterioration of his moral sense, and seems to prefer that the honest man remain and act outside of the government, though capable of influencing public opinion.[27]

We should not dare to say, however, that the differentiation of Pareto is impeccable. In the first place, his point of view is, in my opinion, erroneous. To divide political parties into those that have "arrived" and those that have not or do not wish to do so, is to set up chance as a criterion, unless one considers that there are political parties which have amused themselves in being intransigent out of pure whimsy, which is inadmissible. For if there are parties that, at a given moment, refuse to take office, even when it is offered to them like a ripe fruit, this refusal does not signify a renunciation forever—a thing which would be for them equivalent to suicide. The refusal, on the contrary, is inspired in these cases by the fear either of not yet being ready to assume with impunity the responsibilities of government, or of being uncertain of the obedience of their adherents, divided by differences of opinion on the tactics to be followed; or, again, because they fear accepting but a Trojan horse and falling into an ambush or a trap which their enemies have laid for them. It is certain that such refusals (recent examples have been furnished by the Italian and French socialist parties) may be judged in a very different manner, as approaching a "policy of missed occasions and of tardy repentance." Whatever it is, these refusals to assume power have, as we have seen, an accidental and casuistical political causation, and always imply the party's hope of being able at an early maturity to redeem the mortgage on government and to conquer the state under political constellations more lucky and more promising.

In the second place, by identifying the party "arrived" and the party transigent, Pareto implies a relation between conquest of power and political compromise which certainly can often be verified, but which, nevertheless, is very far from forming a sovereign law capable of comprehending the extremely varied history of modern political parties.

Here, still another question arises. May one, perhaps, distinguish political parties according to whether their aspirations are fixed in past history or in political progressivism? Are there not, indeed, retrogressive and reactionary parties and progressive parties? There resides in this nomenclature a modicum of truth. One can undoubtedly discern parties tending toward a re-establishment of political and social institutions which have existed and which are judged superior and more suitable than the state of things which has replaced them. Parenthetically, we may add that, pursuant to this uniquely historical criterion of time—which involves neither the idea of liberty, nor that of authority, nor yet that of any other principle of political or philosophic order—one should logically designate as retrogressive, for example, the anti-Bolshevist parties in Russia, as well as the liberal anti-Fascist parties in Italy, the monarchist parties of France and Germany, and the irredentist parties in the countries detached from their fatherlands. Of course, this criterion gives us a most incongruous collection of political organizations in which are found joined together mortal enemies bound to one another by but a single tie: their common aspiration toward a pre-existing state of things, whatever it may have been. On the other hand, there is a group of political parties certainly no less incongruous than the collection we have just examined. These are the progressive parties, envisaging a new state of things which has never existed in history, but which they deem possible, desirable, and practicable. The prototypes of these parties are the socialist parties in central and western Europe.

It would, however, not be exact to classify political parties in two categories, those of the past and those of the future. This is true, in the first place, because whoever dares to range himself along with partisans of Giambattista Vico's philosophy of history—the kernel of which consists in the cyclical theory of *corsi e ricorsi*—would not at all doubt the thesis that the present is merely a contradictory parenthesis between the past and the future, with the result that the future often possesses a greater affinity with the past than it does with the present. In the next place, one lacks the historic sense if one supposes it possible completely to restore the past. Epochs of history do not lend themselves to photographic reproduction. In the process, something has been altered, some one has moved, as regards congruity of situation and agreement of will. This is why parties of the past should not imagine themselves able to re-establish the *tempora acta* as they were. The future must perforce be influenced by the durable changes which have been produced, the "reactionary" party must take account, not only of the real advantages evolved by the disliked present order which it is trying to eliminate, but also of the new fundamental interests which this régime has created. Let us cite two examples. In France, the defeat of the great Revolution and of the fulfillment (though incomplete) which it found in Napoleon I, even while involving the return of the Bourbons and the so-called Restoration, did not—despite the promises of indemnity made to the émigrés—at all restore the old great landed estates. The reaction interfered but slightly with the new peasant class, which, through *fas aut nefas*, had been called into being by means of the redistribution of confiscated property of the aristocrats. Although it is somewhat undesirable, and indeed hazardous, to predict a future enveloped in the mists of the unknown, it seems clear that the fall of Bolshevism, uncertain though it be, will end in enormous transformations within the legal and economic constitution of Russia, but will leave intact the new forms of small agrarian property which, at the expense of the nobility, have replaced the *latifundia*.

A word more on the question, terminological in the extreme, of parties called revolutionary. Too often is assigned to the term "revolutionary" special historical significance derived from the memory men preserve of the great French Revolution, which is generally considered the prototype of revolutions. It follows that one attaches the word only to the struggles for liberty undertaken by inferior social classes against their superiors. And in addition to this, the popular interpretation of the term involves the existence of violence and blood-letting; whereas, from the purely logical point of view, the word implies only a fundamental change of a legal order, no matter what means are employed to consummate it. Hence one can sustain the thesis that the terms "revolution" and "counter-revolution" are, after all, equivalent. There is only a moral difference between them, and this difference is merely subjective.

In 1831, a Prussian historian, Friedrich von Raumer, wrote from Paris these sensible words: "For liberals, the word 'revolutionary' signifies the suppression of a decrepit and obsolete social order, pernicious and ignominious; while 'counter-revolution' is in their eyes equivalent to a leaning toward injustice and an outworn order. On the contrary, their opponents, the conservatives, understand by the word 'revolution' the aggregate of all follies and delinquencies; while the word 'counter-revolution' is for them a synonym for order, authority, and religion."[28] It is, then, a question of words that express only sentiments and evaluations, perhaps quite appreciable but entirely personal and arbitrary. Political science should not countenance such kinds of terminology.

Certainly what may appear to some the debacle of democracy and a sad, nearly irremediable, lesion of its eternal principles can seem to others the confirmation of a salutary law. This law prescribes that men, in every enterprise requiring collective action, must submit their particular movements to the rule of the single will of a leader, and that, of the two possible attitudes, loyalty and mistrust, to be assumed toward that leader—to whom democracies must have recourse—the former is the only one that is constructive and generous.[29]

Since the World War, two new parties, inspired by the ideas of Auguste Blanqui on minorities, and still more by the severe and diversified conceptions of the French syndicalist movement under the spiritual direction of Georges Sorel (Pareto's friend), have arisen. These parties have a new basis, that of the elite. Both consequently find themselves in deep-seated contrast with the current democratic and electionist theories. In Russia, bolshevism, while seizing the central power with an unheard-of violence, has imposed on the majority of the population the domination of a proletarian minority. In Italy, fascism, gifted with the same *élan vital*, snatched the power from weak hands and called to itself, in the name of the country, the minority of active and energetic men who are always to be found.

Moreover, the anti-democratic and theoretically minority elite is rather unable to set completely aside the principle of the masses. For more than a century, liberalism, democracy, and socialism have daily addressed themselves to all classes of the people equally. Let us add to this the method of modern patriotism, which we know to be of a revolutionary nature both by its origin and by its tactics, and which has never ceased to attract to it or to try to fascinate the very last molecule of the national community. Indeed, on the eve of the Revolution, France was (or seemed to the democrats to be) merely an assemblage of people badly united, in part strangers to one another. In spite of a constant tendency toward unity, this France of the *ancien régime* appeared to exhibit only diversity, disorder, heterogeneity; to contemporaries it offered the aspect of chaos. France was united neither in civil legislation (which included more than three hundred local systems of law, often contradictory), nor in administration, nor in judicature, nor in military arrangements, nor in communal life, nor in anything at all. Also, in order to voice in this disunited country the sentiment of *la patrie moderne*, one must give to the whole of France, urban and rural, leave to speak.[30] Heaven knows how much she made use of it in the cahiers of 1789.

Now, with the awakening of the laboring and peasant masses which followed thereupon for nearly a century and a half, the phenomenology of the facts which unroll continually before our eyes demonstrates that today the elite is no longer able to maintain its power without the explicit or tacit consent of the masses upon which it in numerous ways depends. There is, then, between the party, monopolistic and so far master of the state as to be confounded with it, on the one hand, and the masses, deprived of so-called political rights, on the other, a social constraint at all points reciprocal. So, at least in Italy, the party of the elite, the Fascists, could but solicit, secure, and conserve the sympathy of the masses. In pursuing this end, the Fascist party was also led by political necessity, i.e., the need of proving to the neighboring states—all more or less imbued with democratic and majority ideas—that, although theoretically a minority, it fully represents the authentic and autochthonous popular will. From this results the adoption of the consensual theory which rests (more than upon the popular vote) upon a public opinion mensurable less by the liberty of the press than by the number of adherents and political and economico-social organizations. It is to some extent popular enthusiasm which serves the parties of the elite as justification of their acquired rights. In relying upon it the party of the elite loses very little of its theoretical purity, because an elite, theoretically sure as it is both of its calling and its power, will, by definition, be self-sufficient. There is no need for the elite to have the majority in agreement with it.

And this is truly the antinomy of anti-democracy, an antinomy not necessarily tragic but dangerous, consisting in a dilemma that appears in a form which one might liken to that of an accordion. For the parties of the elite describe, in their applied political life, a perpetual oscillatory movement, stimulated alternately by fortuities, such as the suitability of the situation, and still more by the two inherent tendencies, that is, by their doctrinaire stereotypes and by their political interests. Indeed, the parties of the elite, turn by turn, swell their structures excessively up to the point of embracing nearly the whole nation and boast of their millions of political and syndical assessed members, and then suddenly contract their frames by expelling the excess, attempting to become again minority parties, properly so called, namely, the parties of election and of choice, sometimes even in proportion to a *numerus clausus*.[81] Between these two extreme limits, the one signalized by the indispensability of the authority of numbers, and the other fixed by the principle of homogeneity and of the strength which flows therefrom, the pendulum oscillates unceasingly.

NOTES

1. Max Weber, "Wirtschaft und Gesellschaft," *Grundriss der Sozialökonomik*, III, 2nd ed., Tübingen, 1925, pp. 167, 639.
2. Friedrich Naumann, *Die politischen Parteien*, Berlin, 1910, p. 8.
3. Maurice Charney, *Les Allemanistes*, Paris, 1912, p. 25.
4. Yves-Guyot, *La Comédie socialiste*, Paris, 1897, p. 111.
5. Roberto Michels, *La Sociologia* . . . *etc*.
6. Charles Rappoport, *Jean Jaurès: L'Homme—Le Penseur—Le Socialiste*, 2nd ed., Paris, 1916, p. 366.
7. Cf., for America, C. E. Merriam, *The American Party System*, 1st ed., New York: Macmillan, 1922, p. 5.
8. *Introduction to Political Parties and Practical Politics*, 3rd ed., New York, 1917, p. 5.
9. Pasquale Stanislao Mancini, "Della nazionalità come fondamento del diritto delle genti," in *Diritto internazionale; Prelezioni*, Naples, 1873; Terenzio Mamiani, *D'un nuovo diritto europeo*, Turin, 1860; G. Carle, *Pasquale Stanislao Mancini e la teoria psicologica del sentimento nazionale. Discorso letto alla R. Accademia dei Lincei*, Rome, 1890; Luigi Palma, *Del principio di nazionalità*, Milan, 1863.
10. Georges Sorel, "Lettre à M. Daniel Halévy," dans *Le Mouvement Socialiste*, 9ème Année, no. 189, tome 190, 16 août et 15 septembre, 1907, pp. 142–143.
11. *La Sociologia* . . . *etc*.
12. Jean Jacques Rousseau, *Contrat Social*.
13. Cf. Roberto Michels, in the *Verhandlungen des Kongresses des deutschen Institutes für Soziologie*, Vienna, September 27, 1926, Tübingen, 1927.
14. *Philosophiae moralis institutio compendiaria*, Glasgow, 1742, Book III, Chap. viii.
15. Vilfredo Pareto, *Trattato* . . . *etc*., Vol. II, p. 248.
16. *La logique sociale*, Paris, p. 297.
17. "Une campagne royaliste," *Figaro*, Aug. 1901–Jan. 1902, p. 32.
18. *Latter Day Pamphlets*, No. 5: *Stump Orator*, p. 167 (Works of Thomas Carlyle, Standard Edition, Vol. III, London, 1906).
19. Michels, "Psychologie der antikapitalistischen Massenbewegung," *Grundriss der Sozialökonomik*, Vol. IX, No. 1 (1926), p. 326.
20. Friedrich Naumann, *Demokratie und Kaisertum*, Berlin, 1904, p. 92.
21. Robert de Jouvenel, *La République des Camarades*, Paris, 1924, p. 69.
22. Daniel Stern (Comtesse d'Agoult), *Histoire de la Révolution de 1848*, Paris, 1887, Vol. II, p. 318.
23. Martin Spahn, *Das deutsche Zentrum*, Mayence, pp. 62–63.
24. *Giornale d'Italia*, April 13, 1923.
25. De Jouvenel, op. cit., p. 66.
26. Pareto, *Trattato* . . . *etc*., Vol. II, p. 638.
27. *Elementi di scienza politica*, p. 462.
28. Friedrich von Raumer, *Briefe aus Paris und Frankreich im Jahre 1830*, Leipzig, 1831, p. 26.

29. André Maurois, *Dialogues sur le commandement*, Paris, 1925, p. 170.
30. A. Aulard, *Le patriotisme française de la Renaissance à la Révolution*, Paris, 1921, pp. 85, 93.
31. Thus the official journal of the Fascist Party on May 22, 1926, carried the following article: "The Secretary-General of the Party deems it necessary to remind all local Fasci that new memberships have been forbidden from April 21, and no cards, whether active or honorary, may be granted. It is intended to block all attempts at adherence on the part of groups or organizations. The Secretary-General insists again that every local secretary must now carry on with great care and energy the task of purging the membership. Only thus can the party with its large membership become a compact and agile organism capable of carrying out the tasks assigned it by the Duce."

CHAPTER VIII

Patriotism

FATHERLAND (patria) is the land of one's father, of one's ancestors, and also of one's mother if she has not changed her abode before giving birth. The derivation finds even more intimate expression in the Italian term la madre patria (mother Fatherland). The Englishman ignores the family connection and uses the broader concept of the region or country (which concept is also found in other languages, in, for example, pays, paese, Land). Thus patriotism, love of the Fatherland, is an attachment to country and to kin. It is of the least value where it coincides with the protection of one's material interests or where the individual uses the whole for his own purposes, for misdeeds committed in the name of the Fatherland are legion. The term patriotism is of the highest value where the Fatherland is conceived as transcendant, as the vessel of the nation, as a sacrifice-demanding superior idea, consisting in the perception of the nation as an eternal thing, surpassing the individual life, encompassing in its needs and interests the future of the unborn.

Love of one's homeplace, "Heimatliebe," springs spontaneously from a personal, concrete, and close familiarity of life and experience with accidental objects (parental home, mountain, valley, tree, dog, echo), the separation from which causes nostalgia. The great susceptibility of youth is the true source and the molder of Heimatliebe. Seen from this point of view, patriotism, with its comprehensive feelings rising far above homely customs and manners, is an a priori abstraction.

Patriotic feelings and Heimatliebe need not correspond to

each other. The former makes demands which may be alien to the nature of Heimatliebe or which may at least contrast with it. It is like the antagonism of two related points of view, which, when observed, differ in quantity and quality. It is at the same time the struggle between nature and politics, between variety and uniform will. Patriotism is the integration, not the dissolution, of regional organization, and it may even gain a new genuine element of strength through diversity in unity. In a certain sense, this element already shows an "international" tinge. For a man with a national outlook, the enjoyment of the colorful complex of national life presupposes a high degree of education and especially of civilization.

Variety is strange to most persons. This factor necessitates that the national state, which is interested in the cohesion of its parts, smooth over extreme differences. In all of these states, therefore, we find the conscious or unconscious struggle against, or the complete disregard of, foreign ingredients and even of native differences. A typical example is the treatment of linguistic dialects in the schools. The drabness of modern life, caused by modern industry and technology, is aggravated by this tendency against "local patriotism." Thus the modern large state and even the small state (in so far as its parts have some affinity for each other) is based on diminished or faded local patriotisms.

The essential components of the extended concept of the Fatherland are: (1) community of race, (2) community of language, (3) community of culture, (4) community of religion, (5) community of destiny and of fate, and (6) community of state.[1]

The community of race or tribe as a basis of patriotism can be only an approximation. It is well known that all large nations and even most of the small ones are a mixture of races; each region even is made up of different races. This is not to mention the fact that most eminent political figures, and many literary ones, are of an alien race (Napoleon, Mazarin, Gambetta, Disraeli, Cavour, Prince Eugen of Savoy—and most of the great Prussian statesmen were not Prussians). This phenomenon has been called the *legge della singolaritá* (law of uniqueness) by an Italian historian. The racist basis of patriotism is denied, with good reasons, by the many Jewish authors of works on patriotism, no matter to which state they belong and even if they believe in assimilating or melting into the host nation. On the other hand, the anti-Semites have championed a racial patriotism, although with little success.

Identity of language favors communication and direct exchange of thoughts and feelings. No wonder, then, that it furthers the development of patriotism. With its cultural superstructure, such as literature and poetry, it widens and deepens the community of culture. The influence of cultural identity upon patriotism can be observed sociologically in two instances: in the fact that in the history of all patriotisms the educated, especially the professional classes, always formed the vanguard and supplied the national martyrs; and in the fact that patriotism increases with increasing education, except where the language used at school differs from that used at home. In such cases, the language used at home usually remains dominant over the language used at school, unless the children involved belong to a poor, dispersed, immigrant group, which cannot possibly oppose the influence of the school. A typical example is the quick language adaptation and Americanization of European immigrants to the United States.

As a rule, identity of language is a main characteristic of the patriotic group. However, even a group with a common language can be split politically by geographical distance, strong economic contrasts, historical dissension, difference of constitution, of political philosophy, and of attitude to democracy. An example of geographical distance is the English and Spanish Americas, and of economic contrasts, the German-speaking sections of Alsace and Switzerland. In the period after the war, nations were again brought closer to each other emotionally by the identity and even similarity of their languages, above and beyond such community of culture as had remained intact. Examples of this are Spanish-Americanism, with its annual joint holiday celebrated in Spain and in Latin America, in spite of the petty jealousy of Anglo-Americanism; Flanders and Holland; and Scandinavianism.

Community of religion may strengthen a patriotism built upon other foundations, especially where nations of different religions exist at the borders. Here, community of religion becomes the differentiating characteristic of the group, even the spiritual core of a peculiar emotional affinity. In times of great religious needs and interests it can happen that a religiously split nation feels this split so deeply that it is led to subordinate its national solidarity to the confessional solidarity with corresponding religious groups of another nation (German and French religious wars of the sixteenth century, Thirty Years War in the seventeenth century). Even in recent times, during periods of weakly developed nationalistic feelings, a common religious faith has the effect of uniting nations to the extent of blotting out identity (as in the case of the Mohammedans) and difference of faith can stifle national unity (the behavior of the Catholic Croats toward the Orthodox Serbs). The World War in many places put an end to the stop-gap principle of religious community as the determining factor in forming nations or even as a nation substitute; in its place appeared a different patriotism, based more strongly on language. This explains the rise of the new Yugoslav patriotism, the separation of the Arabs from the Turks, Pan-Arabism in North Africa, the initiation of an Indian national consciousness which includes the Mohammedans, etc.

Community of destiny is the result of common experience and remembrance in joy and sorrow, wars, defeats, and triumphs, as well as geographic community of space and mutual dependence. Community of destiny is the will of a destiny, which may have materialized as such quite apart from the conscious, spontaneous will of the community, by power of nature or the authority of strong sovereigns and cliques. Community of experience lends to the idea of patriotism a retrospective character. It forms a tradition carried from generation to generation, and it is systematically used by the state through the schools for organizational purposes. Accordingly, a modern Frenchman defines the Fatherland as a form of dominion of the dead over the living. A condition of this retroaction is, of course, that the living acknowledge the work of the dead as living on in themselves forever.

To the modern mind, there is a causal relation of the state to the Fatherland. The thesis of some nationalists that the state precedes the nation in time, is historically unproved. Rather, history shows that nations are first formed on a spiritual basis and then tend to convert the absence or multiplicity of states into a nation state (anima petit corpus). Therefore the claim is made by those who uphold the principle of nationality that each nation should form a state and not more than one (Stanislao Mancini); states without a national basis have always proved untenable in the long run (Austria-Hungary). On the other hand, a national state can make use of the national consciousness which existed, by developing it vigorously through school and politics, and fill the nation with consciousness of the state until one comes to stand for the other. In this secondary sense, the state forms the Fatherland, such as the France of the Bourbons from Henry IV to Louis XIV, Prussian Germany after 1870, and Fascist Italy after 1923. In these cases the state fulfils an educational task toward the nation, which is characterized by MacDougall as a "highly organized group."

The aforementioned components of the Fatherland concept, however, are all subordinated to a further component, subordinated to such a degree, in fact, that they may be wholly or partly replaced by it: the community of will, the will to the Fatherland. This community, subject to the laws of mass suggestion and consequently of variable emotional manifestation, is the decisive one. Its existence can be ascertained and can become the basis of international law when the membership of a group in a nation is decided at a free election (plebiscite). In civil law, this community of will causes individual changes such as expatriation, acquisition of a foreign citizenship, and option, from one nationality to another.

The function of free will explains an individual change of citizenship, along with the corresponding abstract emotions and concrete duties, a change which is usually brought about by emigration and the influence of new surroundings.

The history of the concept of the Fatherland abounds in examples of the revolt of the will against the community of destiny, particularly as the latter can conflict with other, stronger drives like the communities of language and race. The mass emotion which arises from the conflict, and its political and purposeful manifestation, is called "Irredenta." The Irredenta does not deny the necessity for a community of destiny but is rather the urge for a new or renewed community of destiny which presupposes the destruction of the existing one. In this connection, the contention is correct that self-contained states do not know an Irredenta and cannot comprehend its existence in others, while those which are not yet or no longer self-contained are attached to it. In Germany before 1918 Irredenta was hardly known by name and, if it was known it was abhorred, while Italy, the country which originated the expression, has practically lost it since 1918. This makes it clear that the will to the Fatherland appears as the basic principle where other factors are lacking (cf. Ernest Renan's theory after 1870, basing the demand for the return of Alsace-Lorraine on the theory of the Fatherland). The will to be the nation is of course not arbitrary but is itself caused by other elements; in recent times language is among the main ones, although, as has been said, it is not an imperative element.

The possibility of regarding the nation either as a completed or as a continuing plebiscite (permanent self-determination) is quite compatible with the idea of the nation as a creation of free will. Consequently, its right to existence can be thought to be deduced from such a result or situation. Thus the Fatherland is to be regarded as having originated from a re-vocable *contrat social.* No inherent contradiction between emotional and contractual patriotism exists.

The supreme right of the will over all other elements of patriotism, which are merely of speculative character, is proved by the existence of a Swiss patriotism; it lacks any linguistic, ethnic, and religious unity, and its community of destiny is of fairly recent date and has never been forcibly hardened by any acute danger such as war and invasion.

In the political life of the nation, *patria* becomes a party affair. The peculiar political ideal connected with the party causes its adherents to deny to the devotees of all other political and social ideals the mere faculty of patriotic senti-ment. In the eighteenth century only the democrats felt and called themselves patriots; later the republicans did. In the nineteenth century the ruling parties and political systems tried to monopolize patriotism. In the Prussia-Germany of Bismarck, only the parties of the Right were supporters of the state. For William II all grumblers were "fellows with-out a Fatherland." In Tsarist Russia only the conservatives and the Orthodox were "true Russian people." For the Fascist all opponents of his party are "anti-italiani." To the Bolshe-viks, the Russian emigrants are "rabble who prefer life abroad to the reconstruction of the Fatherland." Such value judg-ments are not only products of tactics and tools of a conscious and reckless exploitation of power, but also the most sincere equation of political ideal and Fatherland concept, in which the Fatherland appears merged with certain cultural ideals, philosophies, etc. The concept of the Fatherland of the great defeated parties is the same as that just described. To the emi-grant of the French Revolution, the true France was not in the disloyal homeland but in Koblenz, massed under the fleur-de-lis of the Count of Artois. "France" had emigrated.

The "White" Russians of today, refugees from the Soviet Revolution and communism, do not think very differently.

By strictly separating the means of production from the working masses who work with them and depend upon them for their wages, modern capitalism, also in its peculiar present phase (Sombart's "late capitalism"), has created an international proletariat. In many aspects—in its economic position, and in its anti-capitalist ideology—it shows a high degree of homogeneity, a state of affairs not without danger for the old concept of the Fatherland. For loyalty to the Fatherland can conflict with class loyalty if the value of horizontal ties, which unite class above nation, becomes greater than that of vertical ties which unite the classes in the nation regardless of economic differences. It is then that opposition to the nation can lead spokesmen for the idea of the class struggle to propositions as radical as those set forth by Marx and Engels in the *Communist Manifesto*: "Workers of the World, Unite! You have nothing to lose but your chains!" However, life usually provides a peaceful solution to the conflict because, during international entanglements, the socialist parties which represent the class struggle, turn into socio-patriotic parties. This phenomenon can be explained—besides by psychoses, spiritual compulsion, and coercion—by adherence of the party leadership to the state, on the one hand, and, on the other, by the real solidarity of the working class with its native industry, in whose prosperity they are interested and whose existence may be threatened by revolt or defeat by the enemy. Also, the proletariat of today has more wealth and education.

In a country whose industrial well-being derives from its exports, relations with importing countries affect all parts of the population who have a stake in the manufacture of the export goods, industrial workers as well as leaders of industry and shareholders. It is in the interest of all to facilitate exports, that is, to maintain, and if possible, to increase markets. The sense of producer solidarity against those foreign countries which disturb the process of exporting goods becomes the more compelling, as it is socialist doctrine that teaches that the productivity of the workers rises more and more beyond the buying power of the home markets so that the need for foreign consumption keeps on growing. Thus the worker finds himself dependent on the position of his industry in the world market, and he approaches an imperialist concept of patriotism. This is especially true when the masses are able, by strict organization of their occupational interests, to control the profit of the capitalists to a certain extent and to persist in sharing the booty. The history of English imperialism teaches how well the workers organized in craft unions have understood these connections and have exploited them in their own interest. At the same time a proletarian-sponsored protectionism arises against the immigration of cheap labor.

The preceding paragraphs essentially answer the question whether the intensity of patriotism varies according to property, wealth, or occupation. The propertied classes are tied more closely to the Fatherland than the poor ones. To the former, the concept of the Fatherland is a more concretely integrating part of self-interest. This is also true of the small property-holder. In war the farmer will devote most of his energy to the defense of his own soil; the method of the *franctireur*, the citizen sniper, locally organized, is his most congenial form of patriotism. The tie between property and Fatherland, of course, is valid only if the property is inside the Fatherland. Therefore "international capital," but also international real estate property in land, houses, factories, and such, is more multi-rooted, or, seen from a definite Fatherland, more rootless, than property that does not reach beyond the borders of a country.

Nations are endowed with a sense of eternity. Therefrom spring two patriotic myths: the myth of a Whence, through which the nations trace their origins from legendary heroes or dimly recognizable historical figures; and the myth of a Whereto, which has its root in the collective belief in a peculiar divine or human cultural mission which the nation has to fulfil toward the other nations. Each people believes in some primacy of its own. The arbitrariness of the missionary belief leads to all sorts of encroachments and bloody collisions in international life. On the other hand, it cannot be ignored that the missionary thought keeps nations alive and strong and gives them self-confidence and devotion. It is almost indispensable in international life.

A periodic predominating or submerging of patriotism in relation to the other conscious feelings of solidarity can be noticed and proved historically. The Hellenic feeling for and the Roman consciousness of the state was followed by the weakly political, a-national, universally oriented Christian community of the Crusades, without regard to race and vulgar community of language, but with Latin as the common language of politicians and scholars. With Jeanne d'Arc and through the Renaissance, the beginning national consciousness is deepened in the form of the national state; it is questioned again at times during the Reformation by the preponderance of religious interests, a consequence of the religious split. The epoch of Louis XIV of France yields a strengthened national feeling. The French Revolution again shows strong international features; there develops the struggle of the fraternity of democrats (the patriotic parties of France, Belgium, Northern Italy, Holland, the Rhineland, and Switzerland) against the fraternity of aristocrats (the monarchistic coalition of 1792, and later the Holy Alliance). The nineteenth century consists of a constant change and even a confusion of two trends. One is a national theme, expressed most clearly in the development of the national principle and its transfer to the smaller nations, even down to those that have no history; the other is an international solidarity, alternately based upon democracy (1848!) and Christianity.

To these trends must be added the modern labor movement with its theoretical radicalism whose first historically concrete expression was the founding of Marx's "Internationale." The World War, however, which followed this period, signifies in origin and development the paroxysm of national feelings, splitting nationwise all other ties, socialism as well as Catholicism, Protestantism, Judaism, Freemasonry, and strictly subordinating them to each Fatherland. Soon after the end of the war, there came the revenge of class consciousness, on the one hand, and of pacifism on the other, with a definitely international and partly downright anti-patriotic sting. Against this in turn nationalism rose victoriously in Italy, in the guise of Fascism, while Russian Bolshevism, preserving the international attitude in theory, in practice began to revert to the old Russian national sentiment.

NOTES

1. The student is referred to the following works, among the many pertinent to the subject of patriotism and nationalism:
   Machiavelli, *The Prince.*
   Fichte, *Reden an die deutsche Nation.*
   Giuseppe Prato, *Le Protectionnisme Ouvrier,* Paris, 1910.
   Jakob Klatzkin, *Modernes Judentum,* Berlin, 1920.
   Hans Kohn, *Geschichte der nationalen Bewegungen im Orient,* Berlin, 1928.
   Friedrich Meinecke, *Weltbürgertum und Nationalbewusstsein,* München und Berlin, 1908ff.
   Roberto Michels, *Der Patriotismus. Prolegomena zu seiner soziologischen Analyse,* München und Leipzig, 1929.
   Alphonse Aulard, *Le Patriotisme Français de la Renaissance à la Révolution,* Paris, 1921.
   Esmé Wingfield Stratford, *The History of English Patriotism,* London, 1913 (2 vols.).

Index

Ablancourt, 60(n. 23)
About, 30, 60(n. 9)
Adams, Henry, 9
Adler, Georg, 23(n. 39)
Africa, 45, 58, 117(n. 20), 159
Agnelli, 62(n. 61)
Alba, 53
Alberi, 22(n. 9)
Allemanists, 135
Alsace-Lorraine, 41–42, 50, 58, 158, 161
America, Americans, 6, 7, 27–29, 47, 53, 82–84, 91, 94–96, 98, 114, 117(n. 20), 119, 123, 127, 141, 146, 154(n. 7), 158
Amsterdam, 35
André, 101(n. 33), 102(n. 37)
Antwerp, 35, 41
Aristotle, 4
Arkwright, 83
Arnim, 134
Artois, Count of, 162
Ashton, 83
Asia, 45, 117(n. 20)
Asturaro, 61(n. 39)
Aulard, 154(n.30), 166
Austria, Austrians, 29, 43–44, 57, 90
Austria-Hungary, 43–44, 160
Authority, legitimate, 122–23
Avenal, 72, 81, 83, 86(n. 26, 42, 51), 100(n. 20), 116(n. 7)

Bakunin, 70
Balfour, 71
Barnave, 14
Battenberg, 71
Baudrillart, 87(n. 59)
Bavaria, Bavarians, 70
Bebel, 122, 132(n. 6), 136
Beck, 61(n. 32)
Beckerath, 101(n. 24)
Beckmann, 101(n. 24)
Bein, 61(n. 25)

Belgium, Belgians, 6, 56–57, 165
Belle-Isle, 78
Below, 23(n. 28)
Benda, 112–13, 117(n. 27, 28)
Benoiston de Châteauneuf, 66–67, 85(n. 6)
Bensen, 16, 23(n. 25)
Bergson, 98
Berlin, 36
Bernheim, 87(n. 61)
Bernstein, 22(n. 17), 23(n. 29), 60 (n. 16), 122, 132(n. 7)
Berth, 47, 61(n. 41), 112, 117(n. 25–26)
Bertrand, 62(n. 62)
Bethmann-Hollweg, 134
Biella, 84
Bismarck, 89–90, 100(n. 2), 162
Blanc, 17, 107
Blanqui, 13, 22(n. 12), 151
Blanquists, 135
Blum, 113
Bologna, 39, 137
Bolshevism, 150, 151, 166
Bonnet, 95, 101(n. 29)
Bonstetten, 132(n. 13)
Borghese, 71
Boué de Lapeyrère, 71
Bourgeoisie, see Class, social
Bourne, 100(n. 17)
Boutroux, 124
Brandenburg, 36
Brinckmeyer, 101(n. 24, 26)
Brouckère, 62(n. 62)
Broussists, 135
Bulferetti, 132(n. 9)
Bulwer, 16, 23(n. 22)
Burke, 8
Burnham, 5

Cadet de Gassicourt, 22(n. 16)
Cadorna, 72
Caetani, 71

167

Cafiero, 26, 70
Calvin, Calvinists, 52, 57
Calwer, 59
Candolle, 81, 86(n. 45)
Capitalism, 34–35, 46ff, 91–92, 103
Caporetto, 72
Carle, 154(n. 9)
Carlyle, 132(n. 10), 143, 154(n. 18)
Carnegie, 93, 100(n. 15–16)
Castelnau, 71
Castile, 57
Catalonia, Catalonians, 57
Catholicism, Catholics, 13, 34, 57, 109, 118(n. 29), 134–35, 145, 159, 166
Cavour, 157
Chapman, 83
Chaptal, 50
Charisma, 111, 122ff, 134–38. See also Leadership
Charles-Brun, 55
Charney, 154(n. 3)
Chevalier, 81, 86(n. 43)
Chigi, 137
Choiseul, 67
Choisy, 78, 86(n. 35), 116(n. 3)
Christianity, 165. See also Catholicism, Protestantism, Religion
Churchill, 71
Ciccotti, 56
Circulation of the elites, 4, 63ff, 103ff
Class, social, 11ff, 63ff, 88ff, 103ff
Class consciousness, 15ff, 88–92
Class struggle, 14ff, 88–92
Clément, 50
Clergy, 108; noblesse de robe, 78
Clouard, 101(n. 35)
Cobden, 83
Colbert, 10, 49, 55, 76, 77, 105
Collot d'Herbois, 70
Cologne, 7, 39–41, 86(n. 28)
Colonna, 71
Community, 157–63
Como, 31–32, 39
Compromise, 130–31
Condé, 55
Condorcet, 70
Considérant, 84, 87(n. 57)
Continental Blockade, 38–41, 50
Corsini, 71
Covelli, 70
Croats, 159
Croce, 21, 23(n. 38)

Cromwell, 49, 124
Cunningham, 53, 62(n. 50)
Cuoco, 123
Czechoslovakia, 43–44

Dalton, 21(n. 85)
Danube, Danubian countries, 43–44
D'Arc, Jeanne, 165
Darquet, 96, 101(n. 34)
Darwin, 19, 145
Daudet, 112
Dehn, 61(n. 25)
Delaisi, 96–97, 101(n. 31)
Dell' Acqua, 94
Democracy, 5, 7–8, 47ff, 89–91, 105, 113, 119, 123, 143–46
Demography, 64ff, 103–4
Desmarets, 77
Despotism, 45–46
De' Stefani, 24, 59(n. 1)
Destiny, national, 159–60
Dictatorship, 121, 123, 130
Diderot, 12, 22(n. 6)
Disraeli, 16, 157
Dreyfus, 112
Duce, 123ff
Dumas, 55

Economic determinism, 4, 10ff, 24ff, 107–9
Economic man, 4, 24ff, 96
Edward III of England, 53
Ehrenberg, 101(n. 23, 24)
Einaudi, 82, 84, 86(n. 47), 87(n. 56), 94, 101(n. 21)
Elite, 4, 6, 24, 63ff, 92, 105, 119ff, 151–54. See also Circulation of the elites
Enfantin, 99
Engels, 16, 17, 23(n. 23), 116(n. 12), 163
England, English, 13, 14, 15, 32, 38–41, 48–50, 53, 58–59, 71–72, 89, 91, 94, 98, 130, 164
Entente, 51
Eugen, Prince, 157
Europe, Europeans, 7, 15, 39, 47, 58, 83, 145, 149

Fahlbeck, 64–65, 84(n. 2, 4), 85(n. 17)
Fascism, 97, 113, 166

Fasolt, 101(n. 24)
Fenquières, 66, 85(n. 8)
Ferguson, 12, 13, 22(n. 4–5)
Ferri, 132(n. 1)
Fichte, 166
Fidei commissa, 74–75
Filangieri, 14–15, 22(n. 20)
Flanders, Flemish, 35, 57, 159
Florence, Florentines, 12, 71
Fouquet, 77
France, French, 6, 7, 14, 15, 26, 29, 33, 36, 37, 38–42, 49–50, 53, 55–59, 66, 71–72, 76–78, 83–84, 91, 94–98, 108, 112–13, 127–28, 135–36, 141, 144–52, 159–60, 165
Franchet d'Esperey, 71
Frederick the Great, 128, 133(n. 17)
Freund, 117(n. 24)
Fröbel, 86(n. 54)
Funck-Brentano, 85(n. 19)
Furlan, 85(n. 7)

Gädke, 85(n. 18)
Gambetta, 157
Garve, 11, 22(n. 3)
Geneva, 36
Genius, 123–26
Genovesi, 48, 61(n. 45), 92, 100(n. 12)
Germain, 117(n. 29)
Germany, Germans, 6, 7, 17, 33, 36, 37, 41–42, 46–47, 50, 51, 54, 56, 58–59, 67, 70–72, 75, 78, 90–91, 94–96, 108–9, 115, 125, 127, 135, 141, 145, 149, 159–61
Giannini, 102(n. 38), 133(n. 18)
Gide, 60(n. 9)
Gini, 30, 60(n. 10), 116(n. 6)
Giusti, 86(n. 24)
Goetz, 101(n. 22)
Goetzke, 101(n. 24)
Goldschmidt, 101(n. 24)
Goodness, 128–29
Gorizia, 72
Gourville, 55, 62(n. 59)
Gradnauer, 101(n. 24)
Grandmaison, 71
Granier de Cassagnac, 16, 23(n. 26)
Grenoble, 14
Grey, 71
Grimani, 71
Gros, 96, 102(n. 36)

Grün, 21
Guasco di Bisio, 79, 86(n. 37, 39)
Guesdists, 135
Gustavus Adolphus of Sweden, 64

Hainisch, 87(n. 60)
Halle, 7
Haller, 70
Hammacher, 23(n. 39)
Hamp, 102(n. 39)
Harrington, 14
Heinig, 101(n. 24)
Hély d'Oissel, 71
Hérault de Séchelles, 70
Hereditary rights, 98
Herkner, 60(n. 17), 83, 87(n. 52)
Herriot, 113
Hermsheim, 86(n. 38)
Hervé, 136
Hess, 21
Hindenburg, 72
Historical materialism, see Economic determinism
Hobbes, 14, 92
Holland, Dutch, 33, 35, 37, 40, 53, 55–58, 165
Huet, 10–11, 61(n. 34, 35)
Hüglin, 101(n. 24)
Huguenots, 36
Hungary, Hungarians, 44
Hutcheson, 142
Huysmans, 62(n. 62)

Ibn-Kaldun, 10, 11
Ideology, 19, 26ff
India, Indians, 77, 159
Industrial efficiency, 96–99
Intellectuals, 47, 99, 109ff
Ireland, Irish, 16
Italy, Italians, 6, 7, 26, 38–39, 45, 50, 56, 70–72, 84, 90–92, 94, 99, 107, 114–15, 132(n. 13), 136–37, 139, 145, 149, 153, 160–61, 165–66
Izoulet, 118(n. 29)

Jamaica, 16
Jastrow, 23(n. 27)
Jaurès, 22(n. 18), 113, 135–36
Joffre, 71
Johannet, 77, 86(n. 32, 33), 116(n. 3)
Jolles, 101(n. 24)
Joly, 81, 86(n. 41), 133(n. 23)

Jouvenel, 154(n. 21, 25)
Judaism, Hebrews, 35–37, 158, 166

Kafirs, 46
Kant, Kantian, 11, 89, 100(n. 5)
Karl, 134
Karlsruhe, 68
Kautsky, 117(n. 15)
Kelsen, 116(n. 9)
Klatzkin, 166
Koblenz, 162
Koch, 101(n. 24)
Koenigsberg, 17
Kohn, 166
Kollmann, 101(n. 24)
Kropotkin, 26, 70
Kurella, 132(n. 12)

Labriola, 54, 62(n. 55)
Lacour-Gayet, 133(n. 16)
La Fare, 11, 22(n. 2)
Lafayette, 70
La Fontaine, 76
Lama, 118(n. 32)
Lancashire, 83
Lange, 83, 86(n. 54)
Langh de Cary, 71
Language, 57, 158–59
Lanzillo, 132(n. 4)
Lapouge, 86(n. 25)
La Rochefoucauld, 132
Lassalle, 89, 135–36
Latin America, 159
Laufenburger, 42, 61(n. 31)
Lavisse, 133(n. 16)
Lavrillère, 78
Lavroff, 70
Leadership, 5, 24, 70, 82, 97–99,
    105–6, 109ff, 122ff, 142–43. See
    also Charisma
Le Creusot, 94
Leipzig, 7
Lémontey, 86(n. 34)
Lenz, 23(n. 39)
Leroy, 117(n. 29), 133(n. 24)
Le Tellier, 77
Levy, 61(n. 49)
Liefmann, 60(n. 16), 101(n. 24)
Lionne, 55
Lloyd, 100(n. 19)
Lombardy, Lombardians, 31
Lombroso, 125

London, Londoners, 36
Lorenz, 100(n. 5)
Lorenzoni, 60(n. 14)
Loria, 47–48, 52, 58, 61(n. 44),
    62(n. 63), 86(n. 48), 132(n. 2)
Louandre, 67, 85(n. 9)
Louis XIV, 10, 11, 35, 50, 55, 67,
    76–77, 105, 128, 133(n. 16), 160,
    165
Louvois, 78
Ludendorff, 90
Luther, Lutherans, 52
Lutkens, 117(n. 20)
Luxury, 54
Lyons, Lyonaise, 50

MacCulloch, 12–13, 22(n. 10), 53–54,
    62(n. 51)
MacDougall, 160
Madison, 8–9
Maillebois, 78
Maire, 99, 102(n. 36)
Mallinkrodt, 134
Mamiani, 139
Mancini, 139, 154(n. 9), 160
Mandeville, 92, 100(n. 11)
Mand'hui, 71
Mannheim, 67–68
Marazzi, 72
Marrani, 36
Marshall, 93, 100(n. 18)
Marx, Marxists, 4, 6, 8, 17, 19–21, 37,
    47, 53, 86(n. 48), 91, 107–8, 116
    (n. 12), 135, 163, 165
Mas-Latrie, 71
Maurepas, 78
Maurois, 155(n. 29)
Maurras, 112, 143
Mazarin, 157
Meinecke, 166
Mengotti, 44–45, 49, 61(n. 36, 38)
Merriam, 54, 62(n. 56), 154(n. 7)
Methods, 3, 18–21, 27, 30–31, 54, 59,
    63, 67–68
Meuse, 58
Michelet, 13, 22(n. 11), 87(n. 50)
Michels, 4–9, 22(n. 21), 60(n. 3),
    61(n. 40), 86(n. 46), 100(n. 9),
    116(n. 1), 117(n. 16, 22–23), 154
    (n. 5, 11, 13, 19), 166
Milan, 39
Mill, 87(n. 53)

Millerand, 13
Mirabeau, 86(n. 27), 108, 133(n. 21)
Mirbeau, 100(n. 14)
Mohammedans, 159
Moliere, 76
Montaigne, 95
Montalto, 85
Morley, 130–31, 133(n. 22)
Morocco, Moroccans, 58
Mosca, 4, 6, 47–48, 61(n. 42, 43), 88, 100(n. 1), 106, 116(n. 5), 128, 133 (n. 19, 20), 147
Munich, 7
Mussolini, 90–91, 102(n. 38), 126, 128, 131, 133(n. 18), 136–37
Myers, 60(n. 6), 86(n. 55), 95, 100(n. 19)

Nantes, 35
Naples, Neapolitan, 14
Napoleon I, 38–41, 50, 105, 128, 132 (n. 13), 150, 157
Napoleon III, 50, 84
National Socialism, 115
National unification, 42–44
Nationalism, 156–65, 165–66
Naumann, 154(n. 2, 20)
Negroes, 16
Neo-Malthusianism, 104
Nietzsche, 131
Nimes, 35
Nitzsch, 17
Nobility, 63ff, 104
Non-logical actions, 20, 54–55
Nothaas, 117(n. 17)
Novara, Novarese, 31

Odin, 81, 86(n. 44)
Olivetti, 116(n. 13–14)
Optimism, 140
Orano, 22(n. 19)
Organization, 63, 94–99, 141–43
Ortes, 86(n. 29)

Padua, Paduans, 13
Palma, 154(n. 9)
Pantaleoni, 27, 31, 60(n. 4, 13)
Pareto, 4, 6, 19–21, 23(n. 31–37), 30–31, 60(n. 11–12), 63, 84(n. 1), 103–4, 109, 116(n. 4), 143, 147–48, 151, 154(n. 12, 26)
Paris, 7, 36, 151

Parliaments, 114
Paruta, 61(n. 33)
Pascal, 125
Patow, 134
Patriotism, 6, 156ff
Pavia, 39
Pecchio, 14, 39, 50, 60(n. 24), 86(n. 29)
Peel, 83
Peez, 61(n. 25)
Péguy, 112
Peirce, 123
Philippeaux, 77
Philippe Egalité, 70
Piedmont, Piedmontese, 33, 79
Piras, 100(n. 6)
Pisacane, 70, 107, 116(n. 10)
Plato, 4
Poincaré, 113
Poitou, 72
Poland, Poles, 16, 134
Political class, 46, 106ff
Political party, 5, 7, 134ff, 162
Political sociology, 3
Politico-volitive type, 106, 111, 115
Portugal, Portuguese, 37–38, 49
Power, national, 10, 44ff
Power, wealth as means to, 92–95
Prato, 166
Prezzolini, 62(n. 61)
Proletariat, 80–84. See also Class, social
Protestantism, Protestants, 33–35, 52, 145, 166
Proudhon, 84, 87(n. 58), 107, 116(n. 11)
Prussia, Prussians, 36, 40–41, 46, 89–90, 134, 144, 158, 160, 162
Pullè, 31, 60(n. 15)
Purge, 153–54, 155(n. 31)
Puritans, 34

Race, and patriotism, 157–58
Ramazzini, 13, 22(n. 15)
Rambaud, 133(n. 16)
Rappoport, 22(n. 1), 154(n. 6)
Rathenau, 95, 101(n. 25)
Raumer, 17–18, 151, 154(n. 28)
Ray, 139
Raynal, 45, 61(n. 37)
Reichenau, 132(n. 5)
Reichensperger, 134

Religion, 57, 159. See also Catholicism, Protestantism, Christianity
Renan, 161
Renard, 86(n. 28)
Rentier, 29–30
Revolution, 108, 150–51
Rhine, Rhinelanders, 39–42, 58, 136, 165
Rich, 116(n. 2)
Richmond, 116(n. 2)
Robespierre, 70
Rome, Romans, 6, 10, 44–46, 71, 74, 90
Roller, 116(n. 3)
Rosselli, 116(n. 10)
Rota, 36, 60(n. 22)
Rotation in office, 113, 119
Rothschild, 93
Rousseau, 89, 100(n. 4), 106, 141, 154(n. 12)
Rubichon, 93, 100(n. 13)
Ruling class, see Elite
Russia, Russians, 26, 70, 115, 149–51, 162, 166

St. Augustinius, 135
St. Benedictus, 135
St. Dominicus, 135
St. Franciscus, 135
Saint-Just, 70
Saint-Léon, 117(n. 18)
Saint-Simon, Saint-Simonists, 5, 6, 96–99, 137
Savary, 76, 86(n. 31)
Savorgnan, 84–85(n. 5)
Saxony, Saxons, 39
Schlieffen, 134
Schmitt-Dorotic, 121, 132(n. 3)
Schmitz, 101(n. 24)
Schott, 67–68, 85(n. 11–14), 85(n. 16)
Schulze-Gaevernitz, 60(n. 6)
Schwann, 61(n. 26–30)
Science, 30–31
Sebastian of Portugal, 37–38
Seignelay, 78
Serbs, 159
Sicily, 72
Siemens, 94, 101(n. 23)
Sieyès, 70
Simmel, 25, 59(n. 2), 110, 117(n. 19)
Singer, 101(n. 24)

Smith, Smithian, 12, 22(n. 7), 48–49, 53–55, 61(n. 46, 48), 62(n. 52, 60), 142
Social change, 103ff
Social metabolism, 103ff
Socialism, 91, 107, 163, 165. See also Economic determinism
Sociology of religion, 33ff
Sombart, 6, 35, 52, 54, 60(n. 20), 62(n. 53–54), 72, 85, 86(n. 36, 49), 100(n. 14), 116(n. 3), 163
Sorel, Sorelian, 6, 47, 112, 121, 140, 151, 154(n. 10)
Spahn, 154(n. 23)
Spain, Spanish, 35–37, 38, 49, 55, 57, 72, 159
Spanish America, 117(n. 20), 158–59
Spencer, 89, 100(n. 3), 133(n. 14)
State, 160
Staudinger, 116(n. 3)
Stein, 87(n. 58)
Stern, 154(n. 22)
Stinnes, 94–95
Strasbourg, 42
Stratford, 166
Strutt, 83
Stuarts, 49, 53
Sturzo, 145
Suckert, 91, 100(n. 10)
Suffrage, 88–89
Sulzbach, 23(n. 39)
Sulzer, 84
Sweden, Swedes, 40, 64–66, 69, 85(n. 17)
Switzerland, Swiss, 6, 32, 33, 36, 84, 145, 158, 162, 165
Syndicalism, 121, 151–52
Szabò, 47

Tarde, 6, 81, 86(n. 40), 143
Tariffs, 40, 44, 55–56
Taylor, Taylorists, 96, 101(n. 32)
Thibaudet, 113, 118(n. 30)
Thierry, 16
Thoenes, 101(n. 24)
Thomas, 113
Thyssen, 94
Tietz, 134
Tille, 85(n. 15)
Tocqueville, 13, 22(n. 14), 28, 60(n. 5, 7), 116(n. 8)
Transvaal, 58

Treviso, 39
Trianon, 42
Troeltsch, 52
Turin, 7, 145

Ufermann, 101(n. 24, 27)
United Provinces, 55
Urbal, 71

Valois, 97, 101(n. 30)
Vanderbilt, 60(n. 6)
Var, 16, 23(n. 24)
Venice, Venetians, 44, 71
Vergeot, 101(n. 28), 102(n. 36)
Verri, 12, 22(n. 8)
Versailles, 42
Vicenza, 39
Vico, 4, 149
Vienna, 43
Vierkandt, 133(n. 25)
Villaret, 71
Villermé, 13, 22(n. 13)
Vincke, 134
Vollmar, 70
Voltaire, 35–36, 60(n. 21)

Walloons, 57
War, 40–44, 45, 51, 53, 55–56, 58,
    66–67, 71, 115
Weber, Marianne, 100(n. 7)
Weber, Max, 4, 5, 6, 22(n. 21),
    33–35, 52, 60(n. 18–19), 90, 111,
    114, 117(n. 21–22), 118(n. 33),
    122, 132(n. 8), 133(n. 15), 134,
    147, 154(n. 1)
Weitling, 122
Westphalia, Westphalians, 41–42
Wiedenfeld, 60(n. 8), 101(n. 22, 24)
Wieser, 90–91, 100(n. 8)
Wilbois, 98–99, 102(n. 37)
William II of Germany, 51, 141, 162
Winterthur, 84
Wittich, 75, 86(n. 30)
Work, 26ff, 96–99
Workers, 12ff, 163. See also Socialism,
    Class, social

Yugoslavia, Yugoslavs, 159
Yves-Guyot, 135, 154(n. 4)

Zanon, 49, 61(n. 47)
Zimmermann, 61(n. 25)
Zurich, 36